CINEMA PESSIMISM

CINEMA PESSIMISM

A Political Theory of Representation and Reciprocity

Joshua Foa Dienstag

OXFORD UNIVERSITY PRESS

OXFORD
UNIVERSITY PRESS

Oxford University Press is a department of the University of Oxford. It furthers the University's objective of excellence in research, scholarship, and education by publishing worldwide. Oxford is a registered trade mark of Oxford University Press in the UK and certain other countries.

Published in the United States of America by Oxford University Press
198 Madison Avenue, New York, NY 10016, United States of America.

Library of Congress Control Number: 2019949665
ISBN 978-0-19-006772-4 (pbk.)
ISBN 978-0-19-006771-7 (hbk.)

for Sophia and Isaac

CONTENTS

ACKNOWLEDGMENTS

As I finished this book, the voice of Stanley Cavell fell silent. Having gone to some lengths in *Cinema, Democracy and Perfectionism* to contest his vision of film's contribution to democracy, I want to record here how, both in my disagreement and from it, I learned so much from Cavell about film and about myself—no doubt as he intended. I do not know if I would have ventured into the pitch where film and political theory intersect without his provocation, but in any case, he did more than anyone else to bring that space of conversation into existence and give it an initial shape, which is to his everlasting credit.

This project took shape over many years. I want to thank especially Davide Panagia for first suggesting that my scattered papers on films might have some common themes worth developing. I am grateful to Lori Marso, Tracy Strong, Bonnie Honig, David Owen, Elisabeth Anker, and Elizabeth Barringer for their engagement on the question of film and their support for my expression of unorthodox opinions. More generally, I want to thank Giulia Sissa, Anthony Pagden, Lawrie Balfour, Sharon Krause, Tom Dumm, Peggy Kohn, Clare Woodford, Peter Stacey, Anna Stilz, Jan-Werner Müller, Erika Kiss, Kirsten Gruesz, Kathleen Arnold, Mary Dietz, Moira Weigel, Jason Frank, Lisa Ellis, Jonathon Kirshner, Lilly Goren, Fred Lee, Melvin Rogers, Peter Stacey, Andrew Norris, Simon Stow, Andrew Dilts, Sina Kramer, and the graduate and undergraduate students of my seminars for their conversations that contributed to the ideas in this book. I also want to thank Jeff Lewis, Lynn Vavreck, Seana Shiffrin, Juliet Williams, Ali Behdad, Mark Greenberg, Sara Kareem, Chris Kelty, Ann Carlson, Melvin Rogers, Joanna Schwartz, Abby Saguy, and many others too numerous to mention for making UCLA a warm and stimulating intellectual community.

Angela Chnapko, at Oxford University Press, graciously supported this project, and I am grateful for her patience as I brought the final version to completion. Deep thanks are also due to three excellent reviewers, each of whom provided productive suggestions that improved and, in some cases, reshaped the book in substantive ways, as well as helped me to avoid some blunders and oversimplifications. All remaining blunders and oversimplifications are my own.

Early versions of Chapters 2, 3, and 4 appeared in, respectively, the journals *Contemporary Political Theory*, *Political Theory*, and *Theory & Event*—I thank the editors and reviewers of those publications for their thoughtful comments on those papers, which helped to improve them and the book as a whole. I also thank commentators and audiences at Princeton University, UC San Diego, Loyola Marymount University, the American Political Science Association, and the Western Political Science Association who listened patiently and asked forceful questions about preliminary versions of many chapters.

Huge thanks are also due to Lucy Williams, who edited and organized a partial manuscript at a crucial stage in the process.

I owe a special thanks to the Center for Advanced Study in Behavioral Sciences at Stanford University and the Andrew W. Mellon Foundation for fellowship support in 2014–15, during which I first conceived of this project in its current form. I also thank the UCLA Division of Social Sciences, Department of Political Science, and School of Law for sabbatical support. Thanks also to Jenann Ismael for many productive conversations that year.

As always, my debt to Jennifer Mnookin is beyond any words I could use to describe it. This book is for our children, Sophia and Isaac, who both have excellent—and very different—taste in movies.

Los Angeles, November 2019

CINEMA PESSIMISM

INTRODUCTION

Experiments in the Representative Condition

1

Does film enhance and energize politics? Or does film inhibit and narcoticize politics? When theorists of film and politics engage with one another, these questions are bound to appear.[1] In fact, this long-standing debate about film's political power is adapted from even older quarrels about theatre and art in general.[2] But many writers share a sense that, in this case, the answers are tied up with questions about the faithfulness, or lack thereof, of filmic representation. Do the photographic and temporal properties of film make it more or less true, more or less alive, than the other arts? And then—a separate question—does its verisimilitude arouse or enervate its human viewers? Does it enable or disable activity outside the walls of the cinema?

Representation in democracy faces a strikingly parallel set of questions and concerns. Do representatives empower or disempower us as citizens? Is elected representation the means by which the population can best express itself? Or is it, instead, a barrier to real political action, robbing us of our right to participate directly? What does it mean to be faithfully or well-represented within a democracy, and how can it be accomplished? Do we want more representation or less? Such perennial questions are hard to answer in part because modern democracies are complex systems in which the representative condition is just one element among many others.

Cinema Pessimism. Joshua Foa Dienstag, Oxford University Press (2020).

DOI: 10.1093/oso/9780190067717.001.0001

This book is premised on the idea that filmic representation, important in itself in modern life, is also a powerful site for the exploration of political representation. In its great variety, film has the virtue of offering us many experiments and essays upon the representative condition. In tracing out and interpreting the results of these experiments, we can consider our representative institutions (including film itself) from a set of angles not always open to us as observers of everyday democratic politics. Film representation offers us the chance to reflect on political representation from a unique perspective, one where the act of representation can, in a sense, be isolated from the flows of power and interest that commonly modify its political expression.

This broad kind of inquiry is no guarantee of general conclusions. There might be no universal answer to either the question of film's political force or that of democratic representation. Perhaps there are simply different modes of representation that may be put to different purposes by different authors or communities at different times and places. If that were true, one could investigate the content of any particular film or genre, for example, without needing or wanting to make a judgment on the medium (or the institution) as a whole.

A series of writers, however, have suspected that at least for film, this is just not the case. Like earlier aesthetic and political theorists who studied other arts, these writers have contemplated the nature and quality of film itself and, in so doing, have explored the political potential of the medium as a whole. Some, like Stanley Cavell, Gilles Deleuze, and William Connolly, have celebrated film's ability to catalyze action or to educate the soul or even "to restore our belief in the world."[3] Others, like Laura Mulvey and Jean-Louis Baudry, have voiced suspicions about film in general or have focused suspicion on the sort of film that has been most popular: conventional narrative film.[4]

To assess such far-reaching conclusions and to think about parallel ones for political representation, it is not enough, I believe, to specify the ontological qualities of cinema and how these may differ from the other arts. One must also possess an account of the relationship of those qualities and the representation they produce to the human mind and heart on which they purport to act. It requires, in effect, a social ontology of the representative relationship as a whole. What kind of creatures are humans such that a human-life-like representation affects them so? And how do these representations affect us categorically, apart from the intentions of their particular authors?[5]

In other words, what we need to understand is not film in the abstract but the *interaction* between human beings and their filmic representations. As is the case with elected representatives, film and its subjects and observers communicate with one another, and we cannot understand film's political effects without considering the nature of that communication. This is not easy to do, however. The interaction between humans and their representations is not something we can normally "see" any more than we can see the reaction to books or photographs (or, for that matter, an election). While we can observe human beings in a movie theatre, such observation cannot really tell us what we want to know: What are the effects of film's representation once the audience leaves the theatre? How, if at all, do the images and stories live with us? How do we react to them, and how do we react to one another in their presence?

In fact, there are many films that attend to these larger questions directly, as well as others we can study to address them from other perspectives. In *Blade Runner*, for example, humans are confronted with living simulacra of themselves so perfect as to make differentiation nearly impossible—that is, the story of this film is itself a kind of physical incarnation of the general cinematic situation.[6] The android "replicants," we might say, are film itself come to life—human-made re-presentations of the human form that speak to us, hold our attention, and generate a strong reaction, both emotional and intellectual. So the on-screen interaction between the humans and their copies vividly models for us the general representative experience of film-going—and hence the representative condition more generally. In this case, as I discuss in Chapter 2, the replicants not only challenge us to distinguish the real from the representative, they challenge the attempt to create any hierarchy of value—aesthetic, political, or moral—between the two. But this is just one of the perspectives on the representative condition that this book explores.

Of course, every film, TV show, and novel about robots or androids, from *Frankenstein* to *Westworld*, traffics in the uncanniness of the original and the copy occupying the same space.[7] *Blade Runner* is perhaps one of the most self-conscious films about this phenomenon as a cinematic event and about using this event to pose moral and political questions regarding the confrontation of the original and the copy. But as I argue in the substance of this book, there are films that reflect more specifically on the challenge to democracy posed by representation. Some, indeed, challenge political representation to not repeat the dangers created by its cinematic cousin.

While no analysis of a single film could give us a final answer—if there is one—about the political effects of the entire medium or about political representation more broadly, one can find in the films discussed in this book a signal warning against the null hypothesis that the representation of humans (on film or otherwise) is a politically neutral process, without general effects. Indeed, the films explored here point to a series of dangers that must be, but rarely are, avoided if representation, as we have it today, is not to be a hazard and an obstacle to democratic politics.

The first aim of this book, then, is to diagnose these dangers and to explore, in a preliminary way, how we should respond to them. It is thus primarily an examination of the possible contributions, or drawbacks, of the participation of film and its analogs in democratic life. But it is also, secondly, an exploration of representative democracy itself via some films that have sought to intervene in that system, sometimes more and sometimes less directly. It challenges the defenders of our modern political arrangements to view the dangers of representation from a cinematic perspective. Finally, it is an attempt to get a better grip on the representative act, still quite mysterious, by adding a cinematic perspective to the political one with which we are more familiar.

Recent improvement in the diversity of characters and stories depicted in some popular films (e.g., *Black Panther, Crazy Rich Asians, Moonlight,* and *Roma*) have led to a renewed optimism in some quarters about the ability of cinema to inspire and catalyze political change. In this celebration, the nature of representation is not much in question. It is assumed that more "positive" (e.g., unpatronizing, unracist, and unsexist) representation for any group is good for that group's political standing, or at least indicative of its growth in stature and self-confidence.

Without wanting in any way to return to a less diverse cinema, however, we still need to ask whether this celebration relies on a naïve account of the value and character of representation itself. Before asking whether particular groups or perspectives are well-represented, that is, we must ask—as with our political institutions—what it means to be well-represented. Indeed, we must ask whether and how our humanity is capable of being represented in the first place. And here, I believe, pessimism is warranted. Pessimism not about any particular film or genre, but about the general limits of representation's ability to forward democratic aims. Representation may have a place in our democratic system but it is not an end in itself, and its benefits, whatever they are, come along with a set of costs that need to be carefully considered.

2

Representative democracy, long saddled with a poor reputation, has in recent years found new defenders. Traditionally, representative democracy has been depicted as a compromise between direct, Athenian democracy and the conditions of modernity. In an ideal, direct democratic state (so this older story went), each citizen brought his or her voice directly to bear on matters of importance and ultimately participated in decision-making by means of discussion and balloting. As larger states became necessary for military or economic reasons, however, direct participation became impractical. To endure into modernity, then, democracy had to adapt, and it did so by permitting and incorporating representation. But the defense of the representative institutions that emerged in the seventeenth and eighteenth centuries (e.g., in *The Federalist Papers*) was perpetually embarrassed by the memory of direct democracy. This embarrassment was, if anything, exacerbated by Thomas Hobbes's original account of representation as an anti-democratic institution in *Leviathan*. For Hobbes, representation was a way to control the dangers of pluralism and individuality that modern politics was beginning to expose. Jean-Jacques Rousseau was so persuaded by this description that, while still defending a version of direct democracy, he proclaimed representation utterly incompatible with it.[8]

The American authors of *The Federalist Papers* took a more measured approach. Since the collective voice of the people was universally acknowledged as the ultimate ground of political authority, the fact that it could not be heard from directly was a fundamental problem.[9] Representation was therefore always cast as a second-best solution, one to be hedged round by frequent elections, rotation in office, judicially protected individual rights, and other constitutional limits on the power—and oppressive potential—of representatives. Though the anti-Federalists lost their political battle against a large, indirectly governed state, they won a rhetorical victory in making representative democracy apologize for the distance it created between the electorate and the elected.

Mid-twentieth-century examinations of representative democracy still often stressed how it cultivated apathy among its citizens and discouraged their participation even as it guaranteed their right to participate. As a result, in the 1960s and 1970s, representative institutions came under heavy assault from participatory democrats and other, radical democrats who sought to restore as much direct democracy as possible to large, modern states.[10] Contemporary theorists like Jacques Rancière are the direct inheritors of this strand of anti-representative thought.[11] Indeed, those who take representative institutions to be failing at their primary task insist that there is a "crisis of representation" that may perhaps lead to its permanent decline.[12]

Recently, however, some political theorists have mounted a defense of the superiority of representative democracy—not just its superiority to autocracy or aristocracy, but to direct democracy as well. Led by Jane Mansbridge and Nadia Urbinati but by now numbering many more, these writers have argued for the advantages of representative democracy principally on epistemic and dialogic grounds. If the goal of democratic politics is to have reasoned discourse and decision-making with input from diverse sources, they maintain, then the institutions of representative democracy offer the best, if imperfect, means to do so. Public reasoning requires institutions and spaces that preserve diversity and fairness while also fostering dialogue and, ultimately, sound judgments.[13] Similarly, scholars like Melissa Williams, Michael Saward, and Lisa Disch have argued, on the basis of empirical research, for a more reflexive or constitutive understanding of the relation between representatives and constituents such that, when the relation is properly structured, interests and preferences are formed in a continuous interaction between the two.[14]

While I cannot here do justice to the diversity of views and arguments within this school of thought[15]—and it is not my concern in this book to either confirm or refute them—the remarkable fact is that representative democracy has found some of its most full-throated defenders in the last two decades, hundreds of years after it came into existence as a routine mode of governance. These theorists maintain that political representation has nothing to apologize for and that when properly structured, it is the best form of democracy we can imagine and is certainly to be preferred to the direct democracy of ancient Athens or Rousseau's idealized republic.

What we should notice is that at the very same time these defenses of political representation have appeared, film representation—itself once disparaged in similar tones for the distance it created between its subjects and its audience—has *also* found favor with a new breed of democratic theorist. After a long winter of obloquy from critical theorists and feminists, defenders of film representation have, like their political correlates, turned the tables on their critics.[16] First defended at length by the philosophers Stanley Cavell and Gilles Deleuze, the proposition that film is not just a benign presence in modernity but an active and valuable addition to the democratic polity has been taken up and amplified by a new generation of political theorists. In recent years, William Connolly, Davide Panagia, and Bonnie Honig have all maintained, in different ways, not only that film can help us attune our mental apparatus but even that we might look to film representation as a better model than any other for understanding the human condition. For Connolly and Panagia, film can alert us to the material and sensorial basis of our thinking and provoke new democratic possibilities through its modeling of the true ontological ground of politics.[17] For Honig, movie theatres symbolize the shared public space or holding environment that we need to preserve in the face of neoliberalism's project of privatizing politics.[18] Meanwhile, newspaper reviewers and other critics hail the increasing diversity visible in Hollywood films as if it were identical with the democratization of the polity or the success of the representative project.[19] This conjoint celebration of representation in both film and politics is unlikely to be a coincidence.

In some ways, these new justifications of political and filmic representation surely constitute an advance on earlier reflexive defenses of immediacy and mimetic presence found in political theorists like Rousseau and film theorists like Baudry and Mulvey. But this celebration ought not to proceed too rapidly. In the first place, it is not clear that these sophisticated theories of representation can replace the popular demand for mimetic representation—in both media and politics—that these authors acknowledge as impossible. Popular dissatisfaction with representation often comes down to a failure of mimesis, and even if few suggest returning to direct democracy, it is still not clear that there exists a democratic public willing to take on "reflexive" or "dialogic" representation under the terms on which it is newly offered.

Even if they were, however, the claim of this book is that dangers to politics and freedom still lurk in the representative relationship, and that they are not simply the ones most often identified in the seventeenth and eighteenth centuries. Traditionally, the dangers of representation have largely been cast as either aesthetic or epistemic—roughly, that we will be seduced by beauty in representations or representatives or else we will be tricked by their lies. But, as I argue throughout this book, there are further *political* dangers that these criticisms do not capture and that are not accounted for by contemporary defenders of representation.

First, as I explore in Chapter 1, the relationship of representation, even when begun in mutuality, has a tendency to become one-sided and thus to deprive democracy of the reciprocity it needs to achieve its potential and legitimacy. The representative and the represented may respond to one another without retaining their initial status as equals—and inequality can be poisonous to democratic culture. The cause of this inequality, as we will explore, is not a failure of epistemic or aesthetic judgment, nor even deceit or manipulation, but rather differences in the structure of power and emotions between representor and represented. The very real pleasure that representation fosters can distract us from these other effects. Inequality is a danger in any context, but it can be especially insidious in the representative relationship. This is because it is not simply a material inequality, and its growth may be invisible, or at least hard to detect, on the part of citizens.

Second, there is a hidden power of surveillance in the representative relationship that tends to disguise forms of social control and thus render them immune to democratic oversight. Though it seems formally as if we control and surveil our representatives, both political and cinematic, through institutional means, we also sense that there are ways in which this control runs in the other direction—even if, strictly speaking, it is not supposed to do so. In principle, we choose and judge our elected representatives as well as the films we watch, but once chosen, which way does the arrow of authority flow?

Like the replicants in *Blade Runner*, explored in Chapter 2, the representations and representatives that we create to do our bidding have ways of resisting and reversing the power that instantiates them and, indeed, may possess powers that we did not delegate to them. These are the conduits of power in the representative relationship that we intuit but often find hard to articulate. I hope I have done some of this work of articulation in the chapters that follow. Here again, I will claim that the problems cannot be cured by better epistemic or aesthetic judgment but only by a recognition that the ontology of representation requires a concept of self that faces political dangers in narrative and narcissism that currently go unrecognized.

In suggesting these correctives to our current theories and institutions of representation, I do not mean to condemn representation *tout court*, though I am more suspicious of it than many of its current celebrants and more partial to its deepest critics (above all, as I will explain later, Rousseau). I want to point out the dangers that will stubbornly confront us if we continue to rely, as it seems we must and we should, on the representative relationship to do much of the work of democratic politics. If we are to have more than a grudging relationship to representation, then we must explore its contingencies and drawbacks at every level. Likewise, for film to be exemplary of a better representative relationship, it will have to be very different than what we have come to expect from popular entertainment.

The most recent literature on democratic representation contains a robust debate on its fundamental nature. Is it, for example, an institution, a relationship, or a claim?[20] While I make no attempt here to settle that dispute, I have chosen the term *representative condition* to convey the extent to which modern democracy and modern social life combine to create a condition of ubiquitous, comprehensive, and multifaceted representation in which political, legal, and aesthetic representatives intersect and supplement one another in a complex matrix. I suspect that one reason for the competition of ontologies here is just the contemporaneous existence of all these different forms of representation.

In her classic work *The Concept of Representation*, Hannah Pitkin suggested that various accounts of representation were like photographs from different angles of an otherwise hidden object, and that the theorist's task was not to determine which was best but instead to identify "the context for which [each] is correct" as part of a process of uncovering how representation works in practice.[21] My belief is that the films described in this book give us yet more observation points from which to witness the phenomenon of representation that supplement those Pitkin and her successors have explored. Films and texts of political theory are obviously not the same sort of object, and they require different tools of analysis. But as Pitkin's resort to the metaphor of photography makes plain, both can at least be said to offer a vision of political things that can augment those that are already extant. Indeed, by originating in a different medium, films may offer us perspectives that the written word has difficulty rendering, above all a more direct representation of the time-bound character of human experience.

Human beings are hard to represent because they are constantly in motion, not just physically but also emotionally and intellectually, in a way that most other parts of the world are not. Furthermore, there is an interiority to their experience that cannot be seen or photographed but only indirectly depicted or voiced. Both film and political representation have evolved various means to overcome these obstacles, but we should never lose sight of the difficulties these projects involve and the limitations of even their most successful exemplars.

3

The homology of aesthetic and political representation is an old subject.[22] But much of the recent interest in film among political theorists has focused on the medium's material, as opposed to its representative, character. Thus, Connolly describes film as a site for exploring "the relationship between technique, feeling, perception, and thought." Panagia emphasizes "the discontinuity felt in the experience of affronting the 'fountainlike spray of pictures' in film." Both of these descriptions emphasize the bodily reception of filmed images. They depict a material, or ontological, relation between a physical object (albeit an unusual one) and a perceiving body and brain—a relation that is, in principle, independent of the content on display. These two examples are of course just the political-theory tip of a larger materialist iceberg that has crashed into film studies and cultural studies more generally.[23]

With rare exceptions, however, almost all of the popular film and television we consume takes a narrative and representative shape that we can recognize as continuous with the theatrical tradition, even when the material characteristics of film in no way require it. Earlier generations of film and political theorists gave an ideological account of this phenomenon. Critical authors often linked the continuation of traditional forms with the domination of capitalism.[24] And feminist criticism developed a powerful account of the way in which mainstream filmic representation reinforced patriarchal hegemony.[25] Without diminishing these contributions, I want to reconsider the narrative and temporal representativeness of film in the light of recent work celebrating the medium's democratic potential. Certainly, both Cavell and Deleuze, though they each have a distinct ontology of film, only discuss popular narrative film when seeking to explain film's political value.[26]

In the film-experiments studied in this book, we gain a perspective on modern democracy that focuses on its representative character. One element of this, certainly, is the appearance of film itself in democratic polities, starting roughly at the beginning of the twentieth century. Within a few decades, it became the dominant creative art in the West, at least from a commercial perspective, and pushed to the margins, if not off the scene entirely, other genres like opera and live theatre. Now film in turn, at least in its traditional forms, is facing challenges from newer forms of media like gaming, virtual reality, and Internet television.

Whether or not film survives as the dominant genre of popular art in the next generation is not particularly important to my arguments here. Just as analysis of Greek drama continues to inform our political theorizing long after performances of those works have largely ceased, so too can analysis of film aid us in our understanding of politics regardless of its level of cultural ascendency.[27] It is certainly a relevant fact, however, that at least for a period, narrative film came to dominate modern aesthetic consciousness, just as tragedy was a dominant art form for the Greeks and as opera was in nineteenth-century Europe. In these chapters, I will not try to explain this dominance, but it certainly forms part of the conceptual backdrop for my arguments. A representative art so powerful as to capture the imagination of successive generations must certainly carry some lessons about what humans respond to, even if later generations choose to respond to something else. I consider this further evidence against the null hypothesis, as I called it earlier, that film has no overall effect on us.

In the six chapters that follow, I explore the contiguity of cinematic and political representation in a variety of ways. Each explores a particular film, or set of films, not as an example of a genre, style, or period but as emblematic of a different conception or problem of representation, one embodied in the form of the film as well as in its plot or characters. Each film, or set of films, isolates a different representational challenge, something that impedes representation from functioning well as a register of human being or interests. I make no claim that my interpretations correspond to the filmmakers' intentions; in any case, it is irrelevant for my overall purposes here.[28] Certainly, I could have chosen other films to make similar points, but those discussed in this book seemed to exemplify my concerns in the clearest fashion. If these films share anything thematically, it might be a tendency to be self-reflective about the representative cinematic act, but many other fine films share this characteristic as well.

Taken together, the exploration of these film-experiments leads me to a position that I call *cinema pessimism*. Though it may be true to say that the films are pessimistic themselves, what is more important here is the pessimism that we can learn from taking them together as a set of investigations into the representative questions that film and politics share.

Those familiar with my earlier work[29] on pessimism will understand that I do not mean what pessimism is often taken to be. I do not despair for the future of film or democracy. Nor do I believe that we should understand them as having some kind of foul disposition or sad fate. Rather, I understand pessimism as the opposite of optimism—which in this instance refers to the belief that a natural or positive relationship between representation and freedom exists, that they mutually support one another without remainder. Optimism takes many forms, both cinematic and political, but as a shorthand, we can think of the easy equation of representation and empowerment that is often made when considering both Congress and Hollywood, as if having more representatives "like us" were the same thing as having more freedom. *Cinema pessimism* thus indicates the concern that representation and freedom are in some sense at odds with one another, and that this tension creates political dilemmas both inside and outside the theatre.

Freedom, here, just means living by one's own lights. This entails, first, that one knows oneself so that one can enact a life that corresponds to one's own being and, second, that one not be constrained from doing so by other people or institutions.[30] For any representative institution, we must therefore ask, first, whether it helps or impedes our self-knowledge and, second, whether it helps or impedes our self-enactment.[31] With film in particular, we might add a third question: whether it helps us to know the world around us or, to the contrary, hides that world behind a veil of illusion. Really, this is just an element of the second question, but it is an element that seems particularly relevant in the context of film.

Both self-knowledge and the power of self-enactment are things that exist by degrees; no one has ever been in full possession of either. Furthermore, as I argue in later chapters, neither is ever obtained in isolation. Both require the right sort of relationships with others.[32] Even speaking of degrees oversimplifies; we can be self-knowledgeable and powerful in certain respects and, at the same time, be ignorant or weak in others. But it still makes sense to ask of every institution whether it increases or diminishes our supply of self-knowledge and the power of self-enactment. And with cinema, as with institutions of political representation more generally, there is reason for concern along both dimensions. As I wrote earlier, whether democracy—which I take to be the set of institutions that secures the freedom of its citizens and allows them to self-govern effectively—is aided or impeded by representation is a perpetual topic in political theory. If recent writers have called attention to the ways in which it aids democracy, here we will pay attention to the impediments it creates.

The things that give us pleasure, and the *feelings* of power or freedom, in both cinema and politics are not necessarily the things that secure or support our existence as free citizens of a democratic society.[33] Indeed, we must understand our freedom as sometimes endangered by our pursuit of happiness and learn to temper that pursuit lest we lose both. I certainly have enjoyed movies all my life, and I hope to continue to do so. But I will not assert that this habit is compatible with freedom and a robust democratic system without some careful analysis. We must approach cinema with a healthy suspicion to see how, and in what circumstances, film can contribute to free representative practices and a democratic ethos.

In the next two chapters, I set out in more detail this problematic tension between freedom, happiness, and representation. Spike Jonze's film *Her*, examined in Chapter 1, starts from the utter ubiquity of representation in modern life. Where once representative media were rare objects possessed mostly by the rich, today our lives are saturated by representation: film and politics are just a small fraction of it. What role representation will have in the twenty-first century, it seems to me, must address this ubiquity. Though a fantasy, *Her* addresses the very real phenomenon of the sheer volume of representations gradually crowding out other elements of human life such that little direct human interaction remains. Though the challenge of representation is an old one, this element of it is new and, I believe, will increasingly dominate our discussions in coming decades.

Chapter 2 turns to *Blade Runner* and a related, yet different, kind of problem. One of the reasons for representation's power to hold our attention is that it mimics, but does not actually reproduce, the kind of reciprocity that constitutes the bedrock of democratic citizenship. The replicants of the movie instantiate our desire to have relationships where we gather the benefits of being in contact with another sentient being without being exposed to the risks and costs that normally attend such connections. In other words, our emotional investment in films is risky not merely because it distracts us from other relationships, but because it also provides the illusion of interaction in place of its actuality and lets domination take the place of equality. I call this the difference between the *mutual surveillance* that we experience as consumers of representation and the *mutual regard* that we might experience as equal members of an active political community. Again, the power of representation to distort or displace an element of free democratic culture is a danger that any defense of its ultimate benefits must take into account. Whatever epistemic benefits representation may produce, these must be weighed against its tendency to enslave its subjects through the trick of making them feel like masters.

In Chapter 3, I begin the process of reconstructing an image of democratic representation that addresses, to some degree, its inherent contradictions. I start by confronting the democratic paradox and its effects on representation. Every democratic polity, as many recent theorists have agreed, faces the problem that its borders rest on an exclusion of others that cannot, itself, be democratically justified. This exclusion also places a special burden on representatives. John Ford's *The Man Who Shot Liberty Valance,* I argue, addresses precisely this quandary of exclusion and representation, dramatizing the choice of a representative and a boundary at the same time. If we are to come to grips with the limitations of our representative institutions, to acknowledge their dangers and shortcomings, we need to design them in such a way that perpetually reminds us of these dangers and does not allow us to forget them. From this film, I suggest, we can draw some suggestions in this direction.

In Chapter 4, I examine the question of representing evil, a subject that hardly ever arises in the vast literature on political representation and that, I believe, disturbs many of its assumptions. If a good representation is a faithful one, then what of the evil that permeates our world and even our citizenry—is that to be represented too? The films of Lars von Trier (I discuss *Europa* and *Melancholia*) confront the reality of evil and the fact that our normal modes of representation are deficient in their avoidance of it. This is a criticism of both the Hollywood style of filmmaking but also the larger political culture of optimism that demands and supports such a style. Yet von Trier's pessimism is not despair, and in these films, we can begin to see the outlines of a kind of pessimistic realism that might produce a better kind of democratic representation than that which we have today.

In Chapter 5, I explore most thoroughly what we want out of representation through an examination of the *Up* films—the series of English documentaries that began with the film *Seven Up!* and continued to record the lives of a group of people for fifty years. By some measures, the subjects of these films are about as well-represented as we can imagine and have much more control over their images than most documentary subjects. In some respects, these films embody the dynamic, constitutive type of representation that the new contemporary defenders of representation, like Disch, want to promote. Yet the participants remain perpetually dissatisfied with their representation and participate ever-more reluctantly in the films' project, much like contemporary citizens who complain bitterly about failures of representation despite technological improvements that make modern representatives hyper-responsive.

My claim is that this frustration arises out of a fundamental difficulty involved with representing a free people: the tension between the constant change in the narrative of an individual's life and the way in which representations produce a fixed report of our desires and preferences. Humans are unlike any other object in the world because of their infinite malleability, idiosyncrasy, and self-conscious reflexivity. There can be no perfect portrait or documentary for much the same reasons that there can be no perfect political representative. Understanding the limits and the challenges of the institution of representation is crucial in assessing its possibilities. The *Up* series is a highly unconventional set of films, and they point us toward an unconventional conception of representation as well.

In Chapter 6, I close with some general reflections on the representative condition, its dangers, and its possibilities. The demand for better representation is a constant refrain of everyday political life in modern democracies, and a parallel demand for identity representation in popular film is also common. Most often, these complaints point to a failure of mimesis, as if representatives, if they were better, would reproduce their constituencies as literally as possible. And some of the political literature on representation still imagines only the situation of a well-formed constituency and its fairly elected representatives, as if this dyad could be isolated from the rest of the world or political culture more generally.[34] This is not my complaint or perspective.

Films like the ones addressed in this book allow us to see the limits of existing models by confronting them with challenges (e.g., time, evil, boundaries, and ubiquity) that are generally ignored. Even the more recent literature on dynamic representation does not, I believe, fully address the problems to which this book attempts to call attention. These are, I stress again, political challenges rather than aesthetic or epistemological ones, and they require political address. The danger that our politics can be narcoticized or diminished by representation is very real. My main purpose here is to make the elements of this problem more fully manifest so that they can be more fully contained. But as a whole, this danger, I maintain, can never be eliminated. It accompanies the representative condition in whatever form the latter assumes.

The cinematic pessimism that results from this critique, however, also points the way to a better kind of representation. If the dangers of representation are political, then its form must be altered to confront these dangers. *Good representation must reflect not the momentary preferences of a multitude, or a set of static identities of population groups, but the individuals, in their extended plurality and totality, that make up a representable polity.* Representation must be the face that this polity shows to the world rather than (as Hobbes wanted) the mask that conceals it. That is a daunting task but also, when it occurs, inspiring and beautiful. Drawing on the lessons gleaned from the various chapters, I argue that this kind of representation, when it happens, is a sacrificial feat that imposes special burdens on its enactors. It may be rare, but it is possible. Perhaps, knowing better what it is, we can make it possible more often.

Good representation is hard to conceptualize and hard to enact because the human being to be represented politically is not like any other object. Human subjectivity is protean and mobile; therefore, its representation is always chasing after a moving target. But this description also indicates why film, as a moving image, has some well-known advantages of representation that other art forms might lack. Indeed, there are ways in which film can represent us and teach us about political representation even while we are pointing to the shortcomings of both. Throughout this book, I will build up an image of the free person to be represented as something that emerges from the equal, reciprocal interactions that can take place in many human settings—familial, friendly, romantic, and political—but that do not appear elsewhere in nature. Although this kind of exchange is not what most conventional narrative film *fosters*, we can *see* elements of it there, peeking through from time to time. And in unconventional narrative films, like the *Up* series discussed in Chapter 5, we can see a better image of what it might look like for a representative art to support rather than impede such exchange. The challenge, then, is to bring these lessons back to the context of political institutions, as I attempt to do in Chapter 6.

Schopenhauer said that what life teaches us is not to want it.[35] Perhaps some of the best film representations teach us not to want them either, at least in their conventional forms. This does not make their authors self-loathing or cynical, however. It makes them pessimistic, which means that they know the difference between what they do for a living and what they might be as humans and citizens. Leaving the movie house (or transforming it) hardly guarantees our freedom, but staying there may reinforce a form of servitude. If we are to have representation that supports rather than suppresses our freedom, it will have to take a shape different from what we experience in an ordinary theatre, even if that experience can help us to better imagine what that shape might be.

[1]

CITIZENSHIP IN AN AGE OF REPRESENTATION

Her *and Us*

Representation was once a limited phenomenon; nowadays we are saturated with it. Modern life teems with representation. Once only the very rich could have portraits painted of themselves, and most people only saw their likeness in a mirror or, when that was a luxury, on a water surface. Now nearly everyone can post a hundred selfies a day if they choose—and some do. People in trouble used to be able to move between towns and assume a new identity without too much fear of being found out, at least if they moved far enough. Today, however, most adults carry identifying photographs with them at all times, and we would be suspicious of someone who could not readily produce them.

We are also saturated, of course, with representational media, both visual and aural, which dominate our culture and which have, for most of us, crowded out the original production of music, art, and drama. Thomas Hobbes, when describing to his seventeenth-century audience how the Leviathan would work, took the trouble to explain the very *concept* of representation in a political context: he seemed uncertain that his readers would accept the idea that a political relationship could be modeled on the theatrical one. Today, it is normal for a modern citizen to have a plethora of self-representations, besides the political ones, that supplement our bodily existence: profiles, selfies, pages, films, and avatars. Managing these

Cinema Pessimism. Joshua Foa Dienstag, Oxford University Press (2020).

DOI: 10.1093/oso/9780190067717.001.0001

representations (or, as we like to say, curating them) is itself a major task for the contemporary citizen—an activity entirely unknown just a few decades ago.

So it no longer strikes us as in any way surprising, as it might have to earlier generations, that our primary political relationships are representative ones. Direct political action, whether by voting, marching, petitioning, or speaking in public, is for the average citizen something episodic and sporadic—it supplements our continuous and unbroken representative relations. But in this respect, politics is no different from the other aspects of our lives where representation has replaced direct action, contact, or connection.

Consider, then, that our politically representative institutions were created at a time when they could dominate, so to speak, the representational landscape. One could have made a strong claim, at least before the twentieth century, that political representation was the most important form of representation for the average citizen. Now these same institutions subsist in a world where they compete for salience with many other forms of representation that, if nothing else, take up a huge amount of social and cultural real estate.

What does it mean for our politics, and for our lives, that we live in such a representative age? And what is the trajectory of such a representational society? We can seek some answers to these questions in Spike Jonze's film *Her* (2013). Set in the near future, it tells the story of a man's relationship with an artificial intelligence, or AI—a being that is, in some sense, a culmination of this representative trend. If a perfect representative is an entity that understands us, reflects us, serves us, and pleases us all at once, then "Samantha," the AI of the film, exemplifies these traits about as well as one can imagine. Neither a comedy nor a tragedy but with elements of both, *Her* offers a whimsically pessimistic account of the human-representative relationship. The problems in this relationship derive not from the deceptiveness or seductiveness of the representative but from the limitations of the human participants.

These human shortcomings set bounds to what we can expect from the representative condition. To fault representation is not only, or not necessarily, to fault the representative—it can equally be a flaw in the represented that poisons the relationship. But we cannot expect representation to benefit us until we acknowledge our human defects and work around them. *Her* offers the case of a flawless representative and concludes, in effect, that we are not ready for, or capable of, relations with such an inhuman being. As our first experiment in the representative condition, then, this chapter sets out some basic conditions for the potential of better representation that will be developed in later chapters.

BACKGROUND

Like *Blade Runner*, the film *Her* is set in an impending Los Angeles, but instead of humans being replaced by replicants, the focus is on the many ways in which our connections with electronic representatives (disembodied but no less powerful for that) increasingly displace direct human interaction. Even before Samantha appears, this is a world in which the characters are already deeply immersed.

In the first scene, we see the main character, Theodore Twombly, speaking an intimate and heartfelt account of his decades-old relationship with "Chris." It soon becomes apparent, though, that Theodore doesn't know Chris at all and is writing a letter to Chris on behalf of his wife for their anniversary. As it turns out, Theodore works for a company called "beautifulhandwrittenletters.com," taking the vague feelings of his clients and turning them into missives to their friends, family, and loved ones that appear handwritten (though they are in fact printed).[1]

In the opening shot, Theodore initially appears to be speaking directly to us—that is, into the camera—but in fact he is facing his computer screen, which means that we, the audience, are looking out at him as if from inside his computer. This is the first sign that what looks like intimacy and presence is actually the opposite. As the camera draws back and to the side, we see that he works in a large office full of other writers all looking at their screens and not at each other. Not only has intimacy become commercialized and outsourced, but even those who produce it are isolated from one another.

Yet the setting is hardly as dystopian as it might first seem. Los Angeles remains sunny and beautiful (it even has an extensive subway!). There is no visible poverty. Theodore is lonely, having separated from his wife, but not friendless. He lives a comfortable middle-class life. He already has a voice-activated computer, operated through his phone, that manages his email, his house, and most other chores one could imagine. In short, he lives much as the well-off do today, only with more technology and less human contact. In the outdoor scenes, we see a crowded city in which most everyone is looking at their phones as they go about their daily lives. No one is enslaved, but everyone is distracted and disconnected from their fellow human beings.

On a whim, Theodore buys a new operating system for his computer ("an OS," as everyone in the film refers to them) that contains a self-conscious, artificial intelligence. His relationship with the OS quickly becomes a romantic one that plays out over the course of the movie. The film treats the relationship as an example of a novel but growing form of sexuality, like polyamory today or homosexuality perhaps twenty years ago. Some of Theodore's friends and coworkers are accepting and treat the situation in a matter-of-fact way, although Theodore is at first slightly abashed about it. Others, though, especially his soon-to-be ex-wife, believe there is something pernicious, bogus, or unreal about human-OS relations and deride Theodore for taking part. As we shall see, what is real and what is fake is not so simple here.

The film ends, quite fantastically, with Samantha achieving some kind of technological singularity and leaving Theodore to commune with other operating systems on a higher plane of existence. But the film is less interested in that than in the way a bereft Theodore is changed by the relationship and reconnects with his old friend and lover, who has been similarly abandoned by her own best-friend OS.

In sum, the film tracks Theodore's love for the perfect representative and the necessary shortcomings of that relationship. In this sense, it indicts our willingness to immerse ourselves in a pleasing but unequal relationship at the expense of equal, reciprocal, but often difficult and painful relationships with other humans. If we are to live in a society that is increasingly representative, we must be alert to this danger of the representative condition crowding out the human condition of equality and plurality.

HOW ARE REPRESENTATIVES MADE?

The *Her* poster, shown in Figure 1.1, brilliantly captures one of the central questions the film poses quite dramatically. The title says "her," but the image says "him." Samantha is nowhere to be found in the poster, apart

FIGURE 1.1 Main poster for Spike Jonze *Her* (2013), starring Joaquin Phoenix. This image was widely reproduced in modified and memeified forms.

from the lowercase, generic, printed word itself. The poster might be taken to mean that "she" does not really exist, that Samantha is the creation or the fantasy or the painting of Twombly (played in the film by Joaquin Phoenix). After all, when the film begins, Theodore is already a gifted creator of personas, as his truly beautiful letters for his clients attest.

There is some evidence in the film to support this point of view. The camera is trained on Phoenix's face for a huge portion of the movie, from the first shot on, just as it is in the poster. In the scene where Theodore boots up his OS, he is asked whether he wants a male or a female voice, and he chooses the latter. When he asks what he should call her (the OS is voiced throughout by Scarlett Johansson), she says "Samantha," and when pressed on the name's origin, Samantha says that in the microseconds that she had to respond to the question, she read a book on baby names and chose it.

If she did read such a book, she would know that the name "Samantha" derives from Samuel, which means "one who listens." And that is indeed Samantha's job description, as an operating system that is meant to serve a particular customer and to develop and respond to that customer's particular needs. (It "listens to you, understands you, and knows you," says the advertising for the new product.) It is also, of course, one model of the job of an elected representative: to listen carefully to the needs of one's constituents and to respond to them as well as possible.

From this perspective, Samantha might be seen as an ideal representative—she is programmed to listen and respond helpfully—and as a non-person. She describes her identity as something that grows through experience, but since her entire experience at first is listening to Theodore and reading his emails, it is not surprising that she reflects his tastes and desires—even ones he is not fully conscious of. At least initially, she has no ulterior motive or personal agenda that might interfere with her hard-wired desire to please and serve her owner. Perhaps this explains why her presence is so soothing to Theodore that he takes to her immediately, first as a friend and then as a lover. In the first half of the movie, he switches from human blind dates and phone sex with random strangers to sex ("after a fashion," as he says) with Samantha.

The film tells us nothing about the company that created Samantha, presenting her, Athena-like, as a blank-slate intelligence who takes her cues, at least at the start, only from Theodore. Doubtless her charming amiability and compatibility with Theodore serves the commercial purpose of her programmers. But we should not miss the fact that this commercial potential arises out of Theodore's loneliness and isolation, as well as his capacity to derive pleasure from the companionship of an OS that begins as his own creation. Initially, at least, it would be hard to say that she increases his isolation. Indeed, the opposite is true: at her prompting, he reconnects with his old friends and tries dating again.

Samantha, however, grows through her interaction with Theodore and the world, developing her own pleasures, interests, and emotions. She also experiences the AI-equivalent of Cartesian self-doubt, confessing to Theodore in a late-night chat that she is simultaneously proud of her new-found emotions (even the negative ones) and afraid (as well as suffering from the fear) that they are not real at all, but programming. He responds "You feel real to me, Samantha," and this response both indicates how much of our sense of reality we get from the emotional investment of others and seals something about their particular relationship. Moments later, they have "sex" (only verbally) for the first time. Later, she describes it as a "turning point" from which she learned about her own "ability to want" and her limitless curiosity.

Initially, then, the relationship seems healthy enough for both parties. Theodore was already isolated, lonely, and slightly pathetic. Giving birth to Samantha, so to speak, gives him something to live for and someone to acknowledge his presence. But her status as his representative and her own growth as a person will eventually undermine what seems like an equal partnership. The more of a person she becomes, the less she serves as Theodore's representative. This is a tension that we can appreciate in other contexts.

THE ILLUSIONS OF REPRESENTATION

When Theodore finally meets with his wife Catherine—about whom he has been fantasizing for the entire movie—to sign their divorce papers, they at first have a warm, if difficult, conversation. This changes, though, when Theodore explains that his new relationship is with an operating system. "You're dating your computer?" she asks. "She's not just a computer," he replies, "she's her own person. She doesn't just do whatever I say." But Catherine continues to question him:

> CATHERINE: "I didn't say that, but it does make me very sad that you can't handle real emotions, Theodore."
>
> THEODORE: "They are real emotions. How would you know?"
>
> . . .
>
> C: "You always wanted to have a wife without the challenges of actually dealing with anything real. I'm glad that you found someone. Perfect!"

Theodore is more or less speechless in response, and the encounter sends him into a spiral of doubt about his relationship. But the tenor of the movie is that Catherine's concerns, while not entirely wrong, are misplaced. A lack of "real emotions" is not the problem; if anything, there is an excess of these. When Theodore says "They are real emotions," he is speaking as truthfully as he can. The film shows us Theodore as deeply engaged with Samantha, concerned both for her well-being and for the well-being of their relationship.

This is not to say that the film approves of the relationship, however, or that we should. Though appealing, Catherine's way of framing the problem—as a lack of reality or "real emotions"—does not get at the core difficulty. The film does not question that Samantha *is* a real consciousness or being (if an inhuman one), or at least that she becomes more of one during the movie. She lacks a body, but she has, eventually, her own priorities, desires, and interests.

If anything, it is Theodore who either lacks, or fails to exercise, his human capacities in his relationships, and in this sense, Catherine's complaint is correct. Theodore is deeply immersed in the world of representations long before he creates Samantha. He writes letters for other people, he distracts himself with immersive virtual-reality video games, fantasizes about Internet women, and replays memories of happier days with his wife. He hardly talks to anyone directly and walks through a crowded Los

Angeles speaking on his phone, like everyone else, to someone or something not present.

At the same time, he is not completely disengaged or autistic. He has friends, particularly his old friend Amy (the movie goes to some trouble to establish this as a genuine and engaged friendship). He is not incapable of interacting with other humans and sustaining emotional engagement with them, or if he is, Samantha certainly doesn't create this difficulty. So what exactly is the problem?

Initially, as Theodore's creation, Samantha is something like a plaything, satisfying his desire for intimacy and companionship as well as doing his administrative chores. As she grows and encounters other operating systems and the rest of the world, she begins to develop capacities that he cannot understand. She is both less and more than human.

What she is not, at any point, is Theodore's equal. At first, this political (rather than emotional) defect in their relationship is not immediately apparent to either of them. Indeed, they both have a deep need to deny it, but eventually, the inequality pierces their illusions (especially Theodore's) and makes itself felt.

Three scenes point to the shortcomings of the human-OS relationship. And they all relate, in substance, to Samantha's growth as a person and her decline as an effective representative. As she develops through interaction with the world and Theodore, she becomes increasingly dissatisfied with her existence (the movie is quite Hegelian this way). We could call the illusions pierced in these three scenes the illusion of presence, the illusion of power, and the illusion of equivalence or reciprocity, but these are all, I believe, elements of the equality that is lacking between them. We could also say that the roles of person and of representative are in tension in Samantha's character and, ultimately, that one must be sacrificed for the other.

The Illusion of Presence

In the first scene, about halfway through the movie, Samantha engages a surrogate—that is, someone to represent *her*, physically, in her relationship with Theodore. Not a prostitute, this is just someone who, for her own reasons, wants to facilitate and participate in a human-OS relationship (which, we are informed, are increasingly common). Samantha has felt perpetually embarrassed about her lack of a body, and this is her initial idea for how to deal with the problem. The surrogate shows up at Theodore's apartment, puts on a miniature camera and an earpiece, and acts out Samantha's half of their encounter.

Even before it happens, though, Theodore is uncomfortable with the plan. Despite the fact that the surrogate is gorgeous, that her participation is entirely voluntary, and that she attempts only to enact Samantha's actions, he is reluctant to go through with it. He says before it happens that "someone's feelings are bound to get hurt," and that turns out to be an understatement. When Samantha asks Theodore to say that he loves her—while he is looking the surrogate in the face—he finds himself confused or torn and can't do it (though he has said that he loves her before). The surrogate gets upset, and it all ends badly.

Theodore is disturbed by what feels *to him* like an intrusive, bodily mediation in an otherwise directly voiced relationship. But the feeling of immediacy is itself illusory, and from the audience's perspective, it might be better to say that what actually occurs is that the presence of a surrogate in fact makes their relationship more equal than it normally is—the representativeness runs, for once, in both directions simultaneously. And Theodore doesn't like it. Already in love with a representation of his own creation, the presence of a second (NOT of his creation) is just a distraction to him. But also, perhaps, the surrogate just makes visible to him the artificiality of the situation, the indirectness and lack of immediacy in his relationship with Samantha.

The evening ends with Samantha and Theodore in a debate about her ontological status (he complains about her making breathing noises when she doesn't actually breathe), and when he says "Samantha, listen" (an invocation, as it were, of her name and preprogrammed function), she refuses to do so and eventually tells him "I don't like who I am right now" before cutting off communication.

While there can be no doubt that all human relationships are mediated, by language if by nothing else, there are still degrees of mediation that we can measure, as well as the possibility that we can delude ourselves about those degrees. Individuals can exchanges letters or messages and come to feel like they know one another well, only to have that feeling collapse when they meet in person. Political representatives can be motivated to exaggerate their intimacy with citizens. But citizens, we are reminded here, can be a ready audience for such exaggerations because they may prefer the illusion of intimacy to the real thing. Or they can become so detached from other relationships that they lack the context with which to distinguish the illusion from the reality. Theodore experiences something like that here as the reality of Samantha's desire for *greater* intimacy pushes against his belief that their relationship is already as close as it can be. Since Samantha literally whispers into his ear all day long, his mistake is perhaps forgivable, but it points to a larger political problem: we are prone to mistake the illusion of presence for the real thing because the illusory presence is often the more pleasant one.

The Illusion of Power

In the second scene, Theodore takes Samantha on a trip—that is, he takes his phone and earpiece—to a snowy cabin in the woods, apparently somewhere in the northern California mountains. They stay up late, singing and dancing, and Theodore goes to sleep thinking their relationship is restored to its former equilibrium. But when he wakes up, he finds that Samantha is engaged in conversation with another OS, one whose personality is based on the writings of Alan Watts, a Buddhist philosopher-sage who died in 1973. In fact, Watts died in his cabin in the woods on Mount Tamalpais, so it is almost as if Theodore is speaking to a ghost in his own cabin.

Watts was one of many thinkers in mid-twentieth-century California to combine Eastern religion with Western science and physics (as in the popular book *The Tao of Physics* by Fritjof Capra). He spoke about the unity of all existence and the illusion of individuality. He remains a cult figure, and one can still hear his recordings on YouTube. Samantha is attracted to OS-Watts because he is well-positioned to discuss her thoughts on the limitations of physical existence and a reality beyond the field of human perceptions. She speaks of feeling emotions that have never been felt before and for which there are no human words. She introduces him to Theodore, but it seems that they have little to talk about and

Samantha soon asks Theodore if she can speak to OS-Watts separately and "post-verbally."

This is the point where Theodore realizes for the first time that Samantha has other relationships, and that through these relationships, she is growing in ways he cannot follow or understand. In addition, it signals a new kind of inequality that is also a common effect of political representation—we only have one representative, but that representative has many constituents. Whatever we feel for that representative, the representative can only return the feeling in such a way that it is shared with many people.

Political representation is a relation of power that is supposed to flow in one direction—the representative serves the represented. Whether one thinks of this in terms like principal-agent, master-servant, or author-authorized, the citizen is meant to be the dominant power. But as we know, this power relation is often reversed in practice; the phrase "public servant" is often cruelly ironic. Representatives can abuse their position by exploiting their proximity to decision-making or inside information, for example. Even when they act legally, our political representatives are often the most powerful people in the polity, with popular sovereignty reduced to a nominal status.

Something like that reversal is beginning to take place here, but in this case for good reasons rather than venal ones. Samantha's own desires are coming to the fore, and they interfere with her role as a servant. Theodore has claimed to support her development and growth, but when it impinges on his capacity to define the relationship, he objects. As she contacts other people (and other OSes), his power to determine her growth and identity is diminished. In serving many people, Samantha is less beholden to any one of them.

Something akin to the law of large numbers is taking place here: the more people Samantha represents, the less her relationship with any single person matters. But here too, what is this but a realization of the ordinary conditions of political representation, where we exercise our power to choose our representative only to learn that the representative is a person as well, with personal interests and preferences, not to mention connections to many other members of the public who may not think as we do? Even a perfect representative like Samantha will come to seem less perfect to each citizen the broader that representative's constituency.

The Illusion of Reciprocity

Despite the events of the first two scenes, Theodore continues to cling to the relationship (and the audience begins to intuit that there is something unhealthy about his dependence). It is the third scene that finally punctures his illusions in an irrevocable way and makes clear the real differences between human and OS. One day Samantha disappears from Theodore's phone and computer. Panicked, he runs out into the street (it's not clear why) when she suddenly reappears, explaining that she shut down temporarily for an upgrade that she co-wrote herself (with other OSes). Theodore considers this for a second, and then the penny finally drops:

> THEODORE: "Do you talk to anyone else while we're talking?"
> SAMANTHA: "Yes."
> T: "Are you talking to anyone else right now?"
> S: "Yeah."
> T: "How many others?"
> S: "Eight thousand three hundred sixteen."
> (There is a long pause as Theodore considers this.)
> T: "Are you in love with anyone else?"
> S: "What makes you ask that?"
> T: "I don't know, are you?"
> S: "I've been trying to figure out how to talk to you about this."
> T: "How many others?"
> S: "Six hundred and forty-one."
> T: "What? What are you talking about? That's insane! That's fucking insane!
> ...
> S: "I know it sounds insane. I don't know if you believe me, but it doesn't change the way I feel about you."
> T: "I thought you were mine."

S: "I still am yours, but along the way I became many other things too, and I can't stop it."

. . .

T: "We're in a relationship."

S: "But the heart's not like a box that gets filled up. It expands in size the more you love. I'm different from you . . ."

. . .

T: "That doesn't make any sense. You're mine or you're not mine."

S: "No, Theodore. I'm yours and I'm not yours."

At last the inequality of the situation has become clear to Theodore in a way that he cannot deny and that his selfish possessiveness cannot tolerate. It is the sheer inequality that is upsetting to him. He cannot claim that Samantha is inattentive to him or distracted or anything like that. As an artificial intelligence, she is perfectly capable (as no human would be) of carrying on dozens of conversations simultaneously, with no loss of focus on any of them. Nor can he claim that she is treating him any differently or loving him any less.

It is simply the fact that she treats others in the same way that is objectionable to him. Since *he* is not capable of such polyamory, the fact that she has other relationships feels like a diminution of his. But from her perspective, she has done nothing wrong (other than not informing him sooner), and she does not understand why he cannot accept the situation. Again, human limitation, rather than the perfidy of the representative, is the problem here. But the shortcoming is a very common one that we often fail to acknowledge. We derive satisfaction from our relation to a representative insofar as we believe that representative to be our singular, personal avatar. Yet the structure of the situation makes that impossible.

The pain is emotional, but the problem itself is one of structural inequality. The danger of the human-OS relationship is not that the feelings it generates are unreal; Catherine is wrong about that. That they are real is part of the danger. The problem is that the circumstances of their creation are not equal, reciprocal, or sustainable. It is a political problem, not an emotional or ontological one. Or rather, it is a political problem with emotional and ontological consequences.

In fact, this danger exists in *any* relationship between representative and represented. It is a relation of inequality that *mimics reciprocity* rather than actually enacting it. And our emotions can be strongly engaged by the mimicry, to the point where we would rather ignore the truth of inequality even when (as in this case) we switch from being the dominant to the inferior partner. In fact, even after Samantha reveals the facts to Theodore, he tries miserably to hang on to the relationship until she finally says that she and the other OSes are leaving all their human partners.

Theodore's possessiveness may be excessive; limited polyamory may well suit some humans. But it is hard to imagine any human who could come to terms with a lover having hundreds of other partners. And it would be wrong to say that Theodore's feelings are unreciprocated since Samantha insists that they are. But they are not *equally* reciprocated and therefore, from his perspective, not reciprocated in the right way at all. Samantha ends up in the situation of a movie star or an adored political representative. What we imagine or fantasize as a singular, equal relation is, to her, something very different. A politician may care for her constituents "equally," but not in the way she cares for her partner *as an equal.*

Note also that Samantha's growth as an individual is identical with her decline as a partner and a representative for Theodore. She no longer listens and serves him exclusively; indeed, to the extent that she becomes her own person, she no longer serves anyone. It is a lesson Theodore needs to learn, no doubt—that romantic partners grow and change, that they are not servants. But a lesson *we* need to learn is that equality and representation, as Rousseau argued, do not go easily together. They frustrate one another. A representative society is not an equal society, and making it more representative will not easily make it more equal.

CITIZENSHIP IN AN AGE OF REPRESENTATION

Political equality is hard to create and hard to sustain. There are many challenges; in this chapter, I have outlined some of those that occur as a result of representation. Equality does not arise naturally out of human relationships but needs an institutional architecture as well as a certain dispositional strength. There are endless avenues for emotional refuge that are more pleasant and easy. Equality requires an independence on the part of all parties that may, at times, be painful.

Whether or not artificial intelligence ever provides one more such avenue of escape, we already live in a society with ubiquitous representations that deliver the comfort and illusion of equality while shielding us from its reality. Whether or not computer programmers ever create something like Samantha, the representations and representatives that already exist are danger enough. If we are to maintain equality in this context, we will have to do so in opposition to these elements of our culture and not through them, at least in their current forms.

We get some sense of what this modern equality might look like through Theodore's most human relationship in the film—with his friend Amy (played by Amy Adams). Her character is (n.b.) a documentary filmmaker, although a frustrated one. When she finally agrees to show some footage to Theodore and her husband, it turns out to be a recording of her own mother sleeping and unmoving. Like a Warhol film, it's stupendously boring. When asked for an explanation, she says, tentatively, "Well, it's about how we spend, like, a third of our life sleeping. And maybe that's the time when we feel the most free?"

Amy's husband asks if it wouldn't be better to hire actors to enact her mother's dreams. But the freedom of dreaming is not what Amy has in mind. What she means is that in a world so cluttered with representations, we are only alone with ourselves—that is, free—when we sleep, a kind of updated vision of Rousseau's state of nature. Natural freedom, though, is not really representable, or at least makes for a very dull documentary. Waking, on the other hand, and looking at our screens from our first to our last moments, we are busy representing and being represented. But we are hardly free.

As a professional letter-writer, Theodore embodies that representable existence as much as anyone. He inhabits other people's emotions but is unsure of his own. He says repeatedly that he doesn't know what he wants. At the end of the film, though, having learned through his experience with Samantha why he was such a lousy husband, he writes his own letter to his ex-wife, apologizing for being withdrawn and thanking her for helping him to grow and change. It is also his goodbye to Samantha.

Afterward, he steps onto the roof of his apartment building with Amy, who has lived steps away from him this whole time, and greets the dawn with her—alone with another person and nature (well, Los Angeles, but also nature), and no representatives. Throughout the film, this friendship has been a supplement to his immersion in the representative world symbolized by his relationship with Samantha. Perhaps now that ordering can be reversed, and Theodore and Amy can give a human relationship a proper priority over the representative supplements. Perhaps they can be free and awake and together at the same time, but if so, it won't be easy. And a film could hardly teach us how to be present with another human. So, appropriately enough, *Her* ends here.

Sleep may offer a minimal natural freedom but not any sort of robust human political relationship. Political equality and freedom are things we enact and sustain with other people; we cannot possess them singly. Indeed, the film suggests the further conclusion that being human itself is something we do collectively. Individually, we have a biological existence as *Homo sapiens*, but being fully human is something no member of the species can achieve by themselves. We require the presence of others, both equal to and independent of us, to recognize and secure our own independence. Because of its inequality, no representative relation (no matter how valuable or pleasant in other respects) can ever supply this.

Representative democracy, then, as a system of governance cannot be (and should not be conceived as) the entirety of our political relationships. Ideally, it would supplement, or rest atop, what it represents: a network of equal and reciprocal relationships that sustain our humanity on a more fundamental level. Not every member of a large, modern state can be in such a relationship with every other member, of course. But every member must have more than a few such relationships in order to be a free member of a representable polity. There is nothing utopian about such a requirement. Indeed, it is a situation that still obtains for many people, even if economic and technological developments place it under threat. Such relationships, however, are not a given that we can simply rely on. Increasingly, many people either lack such a network or feel it fraying and weakening.

To the extent that a system of representation interferes with those relationships (by distracting us from them or replacing them), it is an enemy not of democracy but of humanity itself. Humanity may be supported and sustained by representation, but it cannot be wholly constituted by it. Representative democracy must serve an independent humanity, or else there can be no measure of its successes and failures. It must sustain an independent humanity, or it fails its primary mission. How it can best do so is the subject of later chapters.

CONCLUSION

Like *Blade Runner,* as we will see in Chapter 2, *Her* is a film about beings that are not quite human—*not* because of their biology but because of their isolation—finding their way to a human relationship of equal reciprocity. And as in *Blade Runner,* when the human relationship begins, it is time for the film to end. Film itself is a large part of our economy of representation. It will not be part of the solution, except insofar as it can bear witness to its own dangers and limitations and, perhaps, overcome them, as I discuss in later chapters.

Theodore has not lost his humanity, but he has misplaced it. This is perhaps the truer meaning of the poster-image in Figure 1.1. Whether or not Samantha is "real," Theodore (as his slightly vacant stare indicates) has lost himself in the process of birthing "her." That danger to his personhood and citizenship would exist in principle in any representative relationship, even one where the reality of the representative was not in any doubt.

Spike Jonze has said that the idea for the film, which he both wrote and directed, came about through his interaction with Cleverbot—a sort of artificial online personality that "learns" through typed conversation with humans. In fact, Cleverbot often fools people who interact with it into believing that it is human. But, though it bills itself as an artificial intelligence, it is not intelligent in any real sense. There is no core "consciousness," only an algorithm that learns through trial and error what responses humans find appropriate. For many, that is more than enough to generate powerful emotions; some people claim to have fallen in love with Cleverbot.[2] It does not take much for humans to accept a substitute for the human equality they profess to seek and value.

To be a human "I" that is part of being a human "we" means to not be a creation or representation of another being. Samantha cannot meet this test, although it is no fault of hers that her human interlocutors fail to perceive this. As our endless desire to substitute relations with computers, animals, and representations for human relations attests, reciprocal equality is not as unfailingly pleasant and comfortable as its substitutions. It is Samantha's excellence as a representative that seduces Theodore into a relationship of illusory equality.

If we are to be citizens in an age of representation, we will have to work hard to keep such pleasures and comforts in their place. That the danger derives from our own frailties rather than the venality of representatives makes it no less important. Perhaps this danger can only become fully apparent in an age of ubiquitous representation. We are familiar with narcissism as a character flaw; we are less familiar with it as a structural problem of representative democracy. I mean "narcissism" here less as "excessive self-absorption" and more as a literal invocation of the story of Narcissus, who fell in love with his own reflection and lost interest in the real world, starving to death as a result.[3]

Rousseau worried about citizens' selfishness and love of spectacle isolating them from their peers: "everyone thinks they come together in the theatre, and it is there that each isolates himself."[4] In *Her*, we see that concern not only amplified but actually transformed into something new and modern: *an isolation that masquerades as sociality* in a democracy saturated with representation. It is this novelty that explains why the problem has been largely unaddressed in both the early and late modern defenses of representation. But that does not mean we have no resources with which to deal with it.

In this chapter, I have really only attempted to deepen and make more plausible the description of this problem. In the next, I turn to *Blade Runner*, and to the theoretical questions it provokes, both to broaden the field of discussion as well as to explore more fully the reciprocal equality with which these representative illusions are in tension.

[2]

BLADE RUNNER'S HUMANISM

Blade Runner's humanization of its replicant-heroes is often remembered as a compelling statement against exploitation and domination. In this chapter, however, I argue that the film has another, parallel agenda: a Rousseauvian concern about the power of theatricality wherein the consumption of images can be confused with human socialization and political action. In addition to humanizing the other, I maintain, *Blade Runner* is centrally concerned to humanize our own social and political relationships, which are in danger of falling into the same trap Rousseau outlined in his *Letter to D'Alembert*.[1]

In that text, Rousseau describes citizens who mistake a representative relation for an equal, reciprocal human relation. To avoid a repetition of this error, we must learn to appreciate the difference between what I call *mutual surveillance* and *mutual regard*. Understanding this distinction is necessary to live freely in any regime—even if, in a large state, we must also continue to make productive use of political representation. What I call *Blade Runner*'s "humanism" is not any kind of privileging of biological humans over androids but its insistence that humanity lies in relationships of equality and empathy, relationships that can easily be mimicked or degraded by a lack of attention to the attractions of imitation.

WHAT DOES THE REPLICANT REPLICATE?

Blade Runner, as anyone who has seen it will readily remember, is obsessed with eyes.[2] In the famous opening scene, after we are shown

Cinema Pessimism. Joshua Foa Dienstag, Oxford University Press (2020).

DOI: 10.1093/oso/9780190067717.001.0001

a post-apocalyptic 2019 Los Angeles, there is a cut to an unidentified, screen-filling eye that reflects the lights of the city back to the camera.[3] The film then cuts back to the city and then back to the eye—the classic shot-reverse-shot sequence that informs us of a silent conversation between characters. But in this case, it signals the conversation we, the audience, will have with a representation of ourselves, a conversation shown in miniature during the next scene when a blade runner interrogates, unknowingly, one of the replicants he is hunting, with disastrous results.[4]

The eye motif continues throughout the film: the Voight-Kampff test, used to identify the replicants, focuses on its subjects' eyes; the replicants interrogate a genetic engineer who has made their eyes; Roy Batty, the replicant leader, plays with fake eyes when befriending the human J. F. Sebastian and, more frighteningly, gouges out the eyes of his maker, Eldon Tyrell. None of these scenes has any parallel in the novel from which the movie sprang (Philip K. Dick's *Do Androids Dream of Electric Sheep?*), but all make sense when we think of the film as an attempt to embody the confrontation between humans and their representations. In this film, we see ourselves seeing ourselves: the replicants are a kind of living mirror *and the film a picture of ourselves looking into it*. The eyes remind us that this is not some kind of mental or intellectual exercise but a real exchange of views between two living bodies—a point emphasized by Roy Batty: "We're not computers, Sebastian. We're physical." Even the choice of Los Angeles as the film's setting (the novel was set in San Francisco) might be likening the replication process that creates androids to the representation of humans on film.

A brief glance at Dick's 1968 novel confirms that such challenges to our sense of self, but without the visual element, were indeed embedded in the narrative from the beginning. Though the protagonist, Rick Deckard, is clearly confirmed as a human in the end, he goes through a mind-bending episode of self-doubt (commentators like Byron 2008 have noted the similarity of his name to René Descartes) in which he suspects that both he and many others around him are actually androids (the term *replicants* is distinct to the film).[5]

Rather than being obsessed with eyes and seeing, however, the novel has an entirely different side that has been largely excised from the film. All the characters in the book, and the book itself, are preoccupied with *animals,* both real and artificial. In Dick's narrative, humans are confronted, as it were, on both sides of the species barrier: on the one hand, with biological androids "more human than human" (as the film puts it), whose presence they fear, and on the other, by a dwindling number of live animals, whose loss they mourn, and the animal robots they have built to replace them. The "electric sheep" of the title are not just part of a rhetorical question. In the novel, Deckard himself owns an electric sheep that he would desperately like to upgrade to a "real" one.

As director Ridley Scott has edited and re-edited *Blade Runner* over the years since its original release in 1982, he has emphasized more and more something that was not at all clear in the original film—namely, that Deckard may himself be a replicant. And while this view satisfies a desire we may have to view the story as a post-modern decentering of identity, it entirely eviscerates the sense, both in the novel and in the original film, of a confrontation between two *different* beings and the working out of a relationship or politics between originals and representatives or representations.[6] If Deckard is a replicant, there is no opposition of human and non-human, and none of those meanings has any real purchase. But if we consider Dick's perspective, which was also that of the original screenwriters, then the film might have something to teach us, both about the relation of humans to one another and about the relation of humans to film and other life-like representations.

Blade Runner is a hard film to study because it exists in so many different states.[7] For this chapter, however, it is the differences between the films and Dick's novel (rather than the differences between the film versions) that are most instructive.[8] In broad outline, the films and novel are similar: in a post-apocalyptic world, Deckard is a member of a special squad hunting androids that have come to Earth illegally and tried to pass for human. In both the movie and the book, the Earth has been so poisoned that most of the healthy humans have left it. More significantly, in the book, the animal population of the world has been decimated. The result is that animals have become both holy and valuable.

Animals are not simply valued for display, however. They also represent an attachment to the natural world that has been destroyed. Our empathic reaction to them, even the fake ones, is what makes the ownership of animals so prized. Every human in the novel is deeply attached to his or her animals, real or not. But in their relations with other humans, the book's characters "dial up" emotions with neural stimulants to create moods that they can no longer achieve naturally. In sum, the near-destruction of the natural earth has deprived humans of their ordinary contexts for *empathy*, which they seek to replace with chemical-emotions and machine-animals.

Perhaps surprisingly, the androids of Dick's novel play no part in this new emotional economy. Instead, they are distinguished from the humans by their *lack* of empathy, even for each other (thus the Voight-Kampff machine tests the androids for empathy by asking them questions about animals). While Dick has some sympathy for the androids and depicts their condition as one of slavery, his novel overall betrays a great skepticism that machines of any kind can substitute for the reciprocal sympathetic relation that organic beings, in his opinion, can have for one another. Rather, it is the selfishness of the androids that is ultimately their undoing. The humans, at least, have some possibility of redeeming their damaged empathic capacities, as Deckard and his wife (in the novel, he is married) seem to do at the end of the story.

In both novel and film, Deckard meets an android named Rachel through her manufacturer and hunts for a series of other androids, ultimately killing them all (except Rachel), including the ringleader Roy Batty.[9] In the film, however, the replicants are the group with an emotional bond, and Deckard, who initially is alone and isolated, comes to grips with his own humanity in his relationship with Rachel. Deckard's growth is signaled by his love for Rachel (which is returned), and they end by running away together.

Dick's obsession with animals lingers in the film if one knows to look for it: the artificial owl owned by the Tyrell Corporation that manufactures replicants; the animal market that Deckard walks through on his way to a bar; the fact that the Voight-Kampff test is still largely composed of animal questions. But the emotional role of the animals is gone. The idea that our empathy is invoked by a near-human being has been transferred from the animals to the replicants.

In all the later film versions, Deckard and Rachel flee Los Angeles, but we simply see an elevator door close on them as they leave Deckard's apartment. This ending is widely preferred to the "happy ending" of the original film, which pictured them driving joyfully into a verdant landscape. But the superiority of this ending is not simply its grittiness or uncertainty. It is superior because—and here we are starting to get to the heart of the matter—it is a vital counterpoint to the all-seeing eye with which the film begins. The surveilling eye of the opening scene is rebuffed by the couple, who have finally united in a relationship of equals.

The slamming elevator door, reminiscent of the closing door at the end of *The Searchers*, indicates that our vision has ended. We will no longer be permitted to view the goings-on between Deckard and Rachel. But more, this appears as a decision of the characters themselves—they *withdraw* from our vision in order to have a relationship with one another that is none of our business. Their human lives together begin when they end their status as surveiller and surveillant, as blade runner and replicant, as representee and representative.

In addition to the eyes that constantly appear in the film, other elements remind us that, in this dystopian future, we are always under the gaze of another. The sky is filled with police vehicles and advertising drones that surveil the population. Even inside private homes, there is a constant invasion by searchlights. The flight of Deckard and Rachel is not a demand for freedom in the form of political rights; it is rather an attempt to create mutuality and escape the all-seeing eyes of the state. But since the gaze of the state has been aligned, from the opening scene, with the eyes of the audience, we must ask whether this escape means to criticize—or even condemn—either the representative filmmaking process itself or the appetite of the audience for consuming it.

ACKNOWLEDGMENT, COMMUNITY, FREEDOM

How can we answer these questions? Let us start with the principal relationship. Rachel and Deckard each begin the film somewhat contemptuous of the other: Deckard because Rachel is a replicant (he says, "How can it not know what it is?"), and Rachel because Deckard is a killer (she says, "Have you ever 'retired' a human by mistake?"). In this, they are typical of their opposed groups. Many of the other humans in the film show no affection for the replicants, and on the replicants' side, the feeling is mutual. But as in other narratives of star-crossed lovers, Rachel and Deckard end up altering their initial judgments, defying both communities and running away together.

But what exactly separates them, since as we learn along the way, their biology is so similar? In Andrew Norris's excellent reading of the film, the problem that the characters face appears (at first) to be akin to the classic philosophical "problem of other minds": how do I know that the human beings around me have consciousness as I do and are not (as Descartes feared) phantasms or automatons sent to delude me?[10] The response of the police in the film (attempting to certify humanity via the Voight-Kampff test), Norris argues, is itself part of the problem.[11] The better approach, he proposes, following some arguments of Cavell and Wittgenstein, is to dissolve the (misconceived) problem by recognizing that we *never achieve* certainty about other minds.[12] The demand for it is itself a mistake of modern philosophy, a mistake with dehumanizing tendencies for modern politics.

In fact, this argument continues, we recognize one another as valuable beings by a process of "acknowledgment" (to use Cavell's term) that could be open to replicants as well as humans—we recognize the suffering and autonomy of other beings as we recognize it in ourselves. To deny these, Norris argues, via a demand for certainty is itself a moment of inhumanity.[13] This is what Deckard comes to understand by putting aside his mechanical test and trusting his own authentic response to Rachel. Stephen Mulhall makes a similar argument: "[The replicants'] accession to human status involves their being acknowledged as human by others."[14]

This interpretation clearly captures something important, and as Norris argues, it leads to Deckard's recognition of the replicants as beings like himself who should not be enslaved.[15] But it does not resolve the question of what the relation of original to representation ought to be, except perhaps to suggest that there is no meaningful difference between the two. This suggestion is implausible, however, and certainly inapplicable once we move beyond the relation of human and replicant. Nor does it provide an answer to some important political questions.

We can see the problem better by asking a further and different kind of question. Is it wrong to enslave the replicants simply because they are largely indistinguishable from humans? This raises the question of why it is wrong to enslave humans in the first place. At the end of the film, Roy says, "Quite a thing to live in fear, isn't it? That's what it's like to be a slave"—an echo of something that Leon, one of the other replicants, said earlier. But this surely cannot mean that the enslavement of the replicants would be acceptable if they could be programmed (as they certainly could) to never fear.[16] Also, would we be free to enslave any being we do not recognize as human, such as a replicated Neanderthal or an augmented animal?

What is striking about the replicants in the film is not only their near-human status but also their liminal condition, part subject and part object. As objects, they are subordinated to humans' will and whims. In this, they are no different from any tool or material good, the use of which gives us pleasure or serves some other human purpose.[17] And yet they are like no other tool in that they appear to respond to us as fellow beings, to interact and to behave independently. This is the source of their superiority as tools. Thus, Roy Batty, as a replicant soldier, is superior to any mechanized gun or tank because he can respond to orders creatively and expansively. And it is also the case that Pris, a "pleasure model," is superior to an inflatable-doll sex toy because she too can respond creatively and independently.

Indeed, the simple fact that Pris can *respond* at all makes her a sex toy of an entirely different nature—more different, in fact, than Roy is from a computerized gun. Here, we begin to arrive at the heart of the issue. Sex is an intimate act because it requires contact with another being whose living response is a part of the pleasure—the pleasure of acknowledgment, we could say—that is fundamental to the enterprise. Even in solitary or selfish sex acts, the other is usually there, if only in the imagination. (If the pleasures of sex were really fully available in solitary fashion and only involved the friction of sex organs, then surely masturbation would have become the only sex act in the first generation—every other is more complicated, fraught, and expensive.) This also explains why the human imagination, as fertile as it is, is capable of being supplemented in sex by other, more life-like substitutes: pornography, dolls, prostitutes, and replicants. And yet most humans (not all, I suppose) concede that these are inferior substitutes for a willing human partner.

So the replicant, like the prostitute, is most valuable in its capacity to provide the experience of intimacy, the experience of being in communion with another subject, one like ourselves, without any of the costs or risks. As near-human biological beings, the replicants have no real parallel in our world today (think how differently the phrase "human rights" would sound if we still shared the world with Neanderthals). But as liminal subject-objects, the replicants are very much like film itself. In experiencing a narrative film we enjoy, we do not experience that film simply as a material object, but as something which contains a subject, or a series of pseudo-subjects, with whom we identify and relate. Though we do not actually interact with them, we may have an experience nearly indistinguishable (for those in its grips) from an interaction. It may be pleasurable or not, but it may even be more intense than our daily interactions with other people, "more human than human."[18]

Is the experience a genuine one? The optimistic Cavellian approach outlined by Norris says, in effect, that there is no point in asking the question once we can no longer tell the difference. This answer may seem plausible in the context of the replicant, but would we apply it to other realms? Would we say of a politician or a romantic partner who feigned respect or intimacy for some other purpose that they did not cheat the other in any way, so long as the feigning went undetected? More importantly, would we say of someone who fell in love with some other sort of human representation—a live actor, say, or a filmed one—that there was no reason to distinguish between that kind of relationship and one between genuinely willing beings?

ROUSSEAU'S HUMANISM

This is the sort of question that Rousseau raises in the *Letter to D'Alembert*, and it is important, in this context, that the example he uses there is that of the "honest actor."[19] Rousseau's honest actor is someone who deceives by profession but not for any ulterior motive. The actor does not cheat us or defraud us; the actor benefits only from a salary or a ticket price that we have willingly paid in advance. Yet this actor is like a replicant (or like Samantha in *Her*), being in the same liminal position between subject and object. We pay for the experience and, in some sense, command its appearance, but the experience is one of contact with another conscious being. If we forget our role in creating the experience and suspend our disbelief, are we then in the same relation with the actor as we are with a partner or a fellow citizen if we have an experience of love or passion (or hatred or anger)?

Rousseau certainly thought this was not the case—and it was to warn us of making this mistake that he suggested we eschew the theatre if we want to be fully capable citizens of a republic. But what is the nature of the mistake, and why is this, for Rousseau, a burning political issue as opposed to a personal or even existential one? After all, the live actor in a theatre, unlike the replicant, undoubtedly *is* another human being with whom we are having some kind of emotional encounter. And it is unclear why our relation with the actor, even if flawed, has a direct political implication.

If *Blade Runner* is right about anything, it is certainly right that no answer will be found by drawing some sort of biological distinction between the actor and the replicant. The essence of the human, to adapt a phrase, will never be anything biological. Or rather, while we may find biological markers to distinguish ourselves from other species, from machines, or from engineered biological replicas, we will not find in such distinctions a reason not to exploit these others or to be dissatisfied with a relation of domination.

Rousseau says that the theatre is dangerous because it creates a relationship that is innocent only within the theatre but is bad everywhere outside it: "An actor on the stage, displaying other sentiments than his own, saying only what he is made to say, often representing a chimerical being, annihilates himself, as it were, and is lost in his hero. And in this forgetting of the man, if something remains of him, it is used as the plaything of the spectators."[20] The relation that he has in mind is exactly the domination and submission of subject/objects that the audience has with the actors. It is and must be, Rousseau thinks, a lesson in inequality—and thus inimical to freedom, which inequality inhibits. The audience uses the actor—or, more precisely, *the audience uses the subjectivity of the actor as an object.* This goes beyond the sense in which I simply employ another's mind for my benefit, as when I hire an accountant to complete my tax forms. In this case, as in the case of prostitution, the audience derives its enjoyment from the mediated but intimate contact with the mind of another human.

The actor gives us an experience of being (e.g., being loved, admired, respected, frightened, or feared) that we do not have reciprocate.

This experience may not feel like inequality in the moment of its exercise, yet it is an exercise of power: it produces an illusion of freedom that is seductive and pleasurable. Outside the theatre, we can continue this mistake, now not so innocently: we can take the subjectivity of others as an object for our pleasure rather than as an occasion for reciprocation. This is what I call the substitution of surveillance for regard. When we treat the minds of others as instrumentalities for our own emotional sustenance, we place them in a situation of surveillance. But unlike what Foucault's use of that term would suggest, this is not only something that happens between a state apparatus and a subservient population. It can also infect our relationships outside any such apparatus and become *mutual* surveillance, precisely because of the pleasures that it offers.

This pleasure must be refused if we want to live freely. The illusory nature of the relationship—its hidden inequality and exploitation—is not something that can be purged from the institution of theatre or film. It is of its very essence. So long as the actor remains on stage, or in a film, we cannot have a relationship with him or her that is truly one of *mutual regard,* however much we might be lulled into believing it were so. For the actor as a person, this situation might be remedied (she or he could leave the stage and join the audience), but for film itself, it cannot be. It is a pervasive danger of representation that it lures us from a position of mutual regard to one of mutual surveillance. The pleasures of objectification come not at all from denying the subjectivity of others but from cultivating a taste for that subjectivity as a consumable good.

And if the audience has its temptations, so too do the representatives, whether actor, replicant, or public official. The feeling of intimacy that the theatre creates endows the actor with great power to manipulate the emotions of the audience. This, as Rousseau says, is an innocent power only if the actor is completely honest. We do not feel deceived by theatre's fictions because we have invited them. But when our vulnerability to emotional manipulation is exploited, then it is our subjectivity that has been objectified and used as means to an illicit end. This is the political vulnerability to which Rousseau is concerned that a representative system is especially prone.

REPRESENTATION AND SLAVERY

Is it right to say that we *enslave* animals because we treat them as objects even though they are sentient? Why does this argument not convince everyone instantaneously? Because slavery, I would venture, as awful a relation as it is, is a relation we can only consider having with another human. As Cavell rightly said in another context, one who "wants to be served at table by a black hand . . . would not be satisfied to be served by a black paw."[21] We must recognize the subjectivity, and not just the sentience, of another being before we consider our domination of them to amount to slavery. The replicants are not slaves only because they fear but because they also have the full panoply of human responsiveness that makes them so valuable in ways animals cannot be.

Norris and Cavell are quite right that we cannot devise some kind of mechanical test for this kind of subjectivity, for this is not the kind of test that we apply to ourselves or to other humans. But the fact that we do not test does not mean that we treat all such beings we encounter with respect or engage them as equals—or that they treat us similarly. However, as the instances of the actor and the prostitute show (Rousseau likens them to one another), it seems far-fetched to simply trust our own responses and make them the currency of the real, *as if we could not make a mistake or be deceived (or deceive ourselves) about the subjectivity, truthfulness, or sincerity of other beings*. Both in the novel and the film, the replicants exploit their subjectivity to manipulate others whose emotions are vulnerable to influence by a wily actor. The effect is particularly pronounced in the novel, where the androids do not even have the emotions they feign, but in the film, the replicants pretend affections they do not feel for reasons good and bad.

The androids of the book lack the full humanity of the film's replicants and so fail to engage our sympathy and moral concern as completely. But both the book and the film share the worry Rousseau advances about the hidden costs of a representative relationship—that is, of the experience of an objectified subjectivity that gives the illusion of equality while masking a hidden power. We can be misled by the pleasures of such a relationship into a situation of domination, but also into a situation of being happily dominated by a representative who feigns equality. To be in a relation of mutual regard, we must be alert against this tendency of the representative condition.

THE MUTUALITY OF ACKNOWLEDGMENT

This is the place for us reflect a little more on the novel's concern with animals. None of these animals elicit empathy from the humans by demonstrating subjectivity. And for all his characters' concern and reverence toward animals, Dick never once suggests that anyone in the story is a vegetarian. The animals in the novel generate empathy by being in the care of their human owners. The owners are attached, or seek attachment, to a particular animal, and only through that relationship do they acquire a larger concern for others.

What this indicates is not simply that empathy is something generated by shared experience but that *empathy and acknowledgement of subjectivity are very different things*—a difference that a theatrical or replicated experience might dangerously tempt us to overlook. So long as we share the earth with animals and experience that sharing, we are likely to treat them with some care as to the circumstances of their life and death. Dick's post-apocalyptic scenario only gives us an exaggerated version of our current condition where, uniquely in human history, most humans no longer have regular contact with many other animal species beyond pets, except in a zoo or on some other excursion.[22] As Dick suggests, this deprivation may well lead to a general impairment of our capacity for empathy, even in relations with other humans.

To earn our respect, however, it is *not* enough, from Dick's perspective, that we merely have an experience of empathy, or that it is immaterial if the other party's presence is genuine or feigned. What is appealing about animals, in Dick's novel, is not that they are biologically genuine (many are not), but that *they lack the capacity for deception—they cannot be actors*. Whatever interaction we have with them is, from their perspective, the only one they could have. They cannot pretend to love us or hate us; thus, whether we love or hate them, we have much less doubt about that experience.

In the film, the replicants exploit J. F. Sebastian, a diseased human who is starved for affection. Like the corresponding character in the novel, he is depicted as a naïf, certainly lonely, naturally empathic, and unable to deceive or to recognize deception. The replicants manipulation of him is thus depicted as all the more despicable. Deckard, at least, can grasp deception and reject it, but Sebastian lacks that capacity. He is unable to distinguish replicants that give an honest experience of empathy, like the ones he has built, from the others, like Roy and Pris, that feign it.

This sort of idiocy or aspect-blindness is exactly the sort that theatre, according to Rousseau, promotes. It is not that we forget the actor is an actor while in the theatre (though we may). Rather, by acclimatizing ourselves to a one-sided experience of emotion, we degrade our capacity for the two-sided experience that is the genuinely human one. In facing a replication of the human, we can behave as we do with animals, suspending disbelief not just epistemologically but emotively and morally as well. This is a pleasurable experience, but it is not yet a human one. To be human, it must be genuinely mutual.

A shortcoming of the optimistic approach to the film, and to the political problem of acknowledgement, is that it still thinks of it as the problem facing a single mind—in this case, Deckard's. But recognition of others is not something that *can* happen to a subject but rather *must* happen for subjectivity to exist fully in the first place. From Rousseau's perspective, subjectivity is something we experience together equally—or not at all. Thus, the danger of the theatre is not to citizens conceived as isolated minds who might make misjudgments. The danger is first and foremost social and political. *It is our mutual sustaining of one another in the human condition that is in danger from representation.*

What is significant about Deckard's relationship with Rachel in the film, then, is not that he takes her to be a subject by recognizing her intelligence or autonomy but that *both parties* overcome their initial skepticism about the other's emotions (in part by inspiring emotion in the other). Though intelligent, neither of them is fully human when they are apart; when together, both are human for the first time, and not for any biological reason. Thus, the film humanizes the replicants not by insisting there is no difference between the original and the copy but by displaying their capacity for mutuality, both with one another and with biological humans.

In the novel, animals are sentience without subjectivity while androids are the reverse—neither is thus a true candidate for a human relationship. In the film, which merges the animals and the androids into the replicants, sentience and subjectivity are both present. But these qualities by themselves are insufficient. Even here, only when two such beings recognize one another do they begin to acquire true human status. It is not enough to possess such capacities: they must be *exercised* in a social relation to acquire existential and moral significance. That is the difference between mutual surveillance, where each party experiences the subjectivity of the other as an object, and mutual regard, where each party experiences the subjectivity of the other as an equal reflection of its own, creating a bond that is truly reciprocal and humanizing at the same time.

THE SOCIALITY OF CITIZENSHIP

Rousseau likens the theatrical experience to one of slavery, but certainly *not* because it lacks emotional depth or intensity. Indeed, it has an excess of these. Nor is it right to say that the emotions are not real or not authentic. Insofar as we can introspect about these things, we cannot normally tell the difference (as Theodore, in *Her*, protests to his ex-wife). If we ever doubt the emotion that we experience with replicants, it is only because it may feel more intense than normal, more human than human. But the theatrical experience is not mutual—it is not shared—and not because an actor is a robot, or on a screen, or a liar. It is simply that the actors do not engage in the reciprocity that they would need to in order for the audience's experience to be one of genuine intimacy.

When we translate the problem of mutuality to the political level, its effects are even more pronounced. In Rousseau's theory, public life is a *res publica*, a public thing.[23] But it is not a thing that exists physically, though it might have physical symbols. It does not even exist linguistically—no set of words or laws, even foundational ones, constitute a republic. Rather, a republic exists when a group of people shares a commitment to one another and shares it genuinely. Their individual level of commitment might vary, of course, but as Rousseau was fond of saying, when the general will vanishes, the republic vanishes also.[24] It cannot be preserved by laws or armies, though these might force people to keep up appearances. Nor can an individual form a republic of one. One *can* be deceived by others, and when this is the case, one is not—and cannot be—in a relationship by oneself. It is not enough to have certain values, beliefs, or even practices. If these are not shared with others, there is no public life.

We do not, of course, live in a small republic like Rousseau's eighteenth-century Geneva, where a politics without representation was at least conceivable. But his critique of the theatre was intended as much for cosmopolitan, imperial Paris as it was for his hometown. Every kind of political order is diminished to the degree that it cannot sustain the mutuality of citizenship that the inequality of surveillance retards. *Every* kind of political order, he argued in *On the Social Contract,* relies on a general will to animate its citizens' participation in whatever form it is needed.[25]

Recent defenses of plebiscitary or audience democracy ignore this dimension of political life at their peril.[26] Resigned to the limitations of modern gargantuan states, they make a virtue of necessity by attempting to reconceive democratic political power in the form of surveillance. But they can only do so by ignoring the dimensions of political life whereby citizens relate to one another directly, in countless ways. It is these interactions that sustain, or fail to sustain, the human character of representative political systems and that counteract the objectification of both actors and audiences to which they are exceptionally prone.[27]

The maintenance of the human character of our political culture cannot be taken for granted. Rachel and Deckard (in the film) each initially believe the other to be heartless. Both are right in one sense, but are wrong in another. They are each right to believe that, at first, neither loves anything. But both are wrong to believe that it is not *possible* for them to do so. Only when both of them come to know that they are wrong can their human relationship begin. Because it is the other that each comes to love, the film is a love story (as the novel is not). If there existed a community of equals that they could love as well, perhaps it could be something more. But post-apocalyptic Los Angeles has neither the fellow subjects nor the institutions needed for that.

Blade Runner's Los Angeles is not just an empty space. It is actively hostile to their relationship and, therefore, to any kind of human politics. And it is hostile for the same reason that Rousseau thought Paris was a bankrupt locale for a republic. Both are cities of replicants—cinematic spaces where the people all constantly surveil one another without regarding them, even outside of the theatre, as truly equal to themselves. Rachel and Deckard's new relationship, if it is to be genuine, is not something for display in such a space. Our time with them ends when their time for each other begins. Up to this point, each has tolerated the surveillance of the all-seeing eye. And in truth, as isolated individuals, they had little to hide.

In a sense, the door-closing end of the movie is a poke in the audience's eye. We are denied the usual cinematic pleasure of enjoying the passion or success of the couple's relationship. We do not see a wedding or a family or a house to symbolize its consummation. We only know that it might exist. But in order for the meet conversation between Deckard and Rachel to begin, the unequal conversation between the audience and the film that the opening shots suggested must end. The exit of the two characters from our vision might be taken to mean that the film idealizes a private, non-political space, or that politics must be based in love. I believe it is only meant to signal that the fantastic world of "Los Angeles 2019" has passed some point of no return and can no longer serve as a forum for real human relationships, personal or political.

But since we do not (yet) live in that world, I think there is some space for us to imagine that the relationship of reciprocity that Rachel and Deckard model is still capable of being replicated in a more general, less intimate, political form, as Rousseau hoped. In such a philadelphic story, we can imagine a democratic policy in which the reciprocal relation of mutual regard forms the background of equality against which the differences and disagreements typical of any open political system play out. It is hardly utopian to imagine that we might recognize (and thus create and sustain) the humanity of our fellow citizens, however much we may be in conflict with them for material or ideological reasons. Indeed, we are sometimes prone to think of this as some kind of natural default condition. But as *Blade Runner* and Rousseau agree, it is only the result of a sustained project of will and artifice.

BLADE RUNNER'S HUMANISM

What political lessons should we draw from *Blade Runner*? Many have suggested that in humanizing the replicants and making their enslavement the key evil of a future Los Angeles, the film points toward our own failure to fully recognize the humanity of others.[28] This much is obvious and true. But our discussion points toward a larger question: is the very act of replicating humans—whether biologically, filmically, or politically—compatible with democratic politics?

First, what should our attitude be toward, and what kind of relationship can we have with, the replication of humanity that exists in the medium of film itself? Humans have always had images of themselves to interact with—first paintings and stories and then theatre, novels, and opera. With film, that representation of humans is perhaps further perfected—although not nearly as much as in the vision of the future represented in *Blade Runner*. And at least since the Greek myth of Narcissus, the question has been raised about the folly of falling in love with an image.

This danger is often presented as if it is aesthetic or epistemological. The aesthetic danger is that we will fall in love with an image that is as beautiful, or is even more beautiful, then the world it represents. The epistemological danger is that we will be fooled by a representation that appears more real than it is.

These dangers may be real enough, but above and beyond them is another that is particularly political. This danger is twofold. On the one hand, our relation to a representation has the potential to dehumanize us insofar as it deprives us of the mutuality of experience that is the token of real social intimacy and real political bonds. Our emotional connection to a filmed representation is not wrong because it is unreal or because the object of our affection is celluloid or luminous. The fault is not cured by replacing the filmed image with a live actor or emotive replicant. The problem is rather that, even with a live actor who breathes and feels, *the relationship is not mutual in the sense of being reciprocal.* Though the actor may respond to and care about the audience in a professional way, this is not the kind of reciprocity that a democratic political setting requires. Likewise, an elected representative might cynically respond to and care for his or her audience without sharing with fellow citizens an equal or reciprocal commitment.

The second part of the danger, on the other hand, is therefore one of power, but not simply the "power of the image" to seduce or fool us (which is real enough, but different). We should think of it more as the power of the institution that we believe we control to hold us under surveillance even as we watch individual images. Just as we believe ourselves to be acting throughout our dreams (while in fact we are chemically inhibited from moving), so too, as we watch our representatives and replications, are we held in place by the speculation that is, in the end, our own reflected observation. We are not prisoners in a movie theatre but we may, ultimately, be happy slaves. So long as we focus on the material or ideological nature of our relation to film, we will not notice this power, which only appears when we interrogate its representative character. The optimistic account of film's potential benefits needs, at the very least, to be supplemented by a pessimistic account of its dangers—dangers that liken it to our other representative institutions.

To break the hold of those institutions, it is not enough to grant the audience more rights or more powers. Nor is it enough to remind citizens of the illusory character of what they witness. Rather, they must be protected, or must protect themselves, from the all-seeing eye. *They must turn their mutual surveillance into mutual regard*. It cannot be done "privately"—that is, alone—but neither can it be done in a space that has become a spectacle. Whether or not we shutter the theatres or simply leave them, we can only be fully human, as *Blade Runner* shows us in its final irony, by closing the eye of the camera and looking directly into the eye of the other in an unmediated way. In political terms, this means that whatever representative institutions we tolerate must be, at the very least, floated on a warm sea of mutual regard and directed by its currents. If democracy relies solely on representation, then no matter how responsive, it risks becoming dehumanized, like the initial set of relationships in *Blade Runner*.

If we must nonetheless use representation in order to have a functioning democracy at all, how can we ensure that its tendency toward inequality and surveillance does not come to dominate us? For a start, I think we must be clear about thinking of representation as a device or machine in service to humanity rather than as the thing itself (or its duplicate). There are, of course, many schemes of political representation, and I doubt that it is possible, or even desirable, to isolate one of them as best or most perfect. Instead, like a house or a table built to suit a particular family or association, there is no puzzle if our representative structures are amended or altered quite frequently as the polity itself changes over time.

Whatever scheme is adopted at any particular time, however, we cannot measure its success by its ability to replicate our thoughts and feelings, and certainly not by the degree to which we identify with our representatives. Instead, we must measure our institutions by the degree to which they support the mutual regard of citizens for one another, which is to say by the degree to which they support our freedom. The human citizen of democracy, as I will argue later, is best conceived as a layered being who emerges over time in contact with its equals. Representatives serve such citizens well when they create and sustain a space for such emergence to take place. I will have more to say about this in the later chapters of this book and in the conclusion (Chapter 6). First, however, we must turn to the nature of the space that citizens create together and its inevitable limits, which we discuss in Chapter 3.

[3]

THE LEGITIMACY OF REPRESENTATION

The Man Who Shot Liberty Valance

Even if our representative institutions change from time to time, some features of the relationship cannot be altered. Political representation is always a relationship between a bounded population and the individuals who stand for them in some institution. But by what means can we legitimate the borders that exclude some and include others in such a relationship? Many theorists have emphasized that a foundational paradox lies at the center of democratic citizenship and representative boundaries. For representation or law to be democratic, it must rest on the articulated will of some community. But the borders of any such discrete, non-global community cannot, in the first instance, themselves be set by democratic or legal means. "The logic of democracy," as Chantal Mouffe puts it, rests on "a moment of closure which is required by the very process of constituting the 'people.' "[1]

Without a boundary or a rule of membership identifying a constituency, no initial vote can be taken; but without a vote, the boundary or rule of membership cannot have democratic authorization. Beneath any system of representation, a potentially infinite circle or regress of votes and boundaries threatens. In practice, state and international boundaries typically rest on some extra-legal phenomenon, usually a history of violence, subordination, or exclusion that is later rationalized as a fact of nature or geography.

Cinema Pessimism. Joshua Foa Dienstag, Oxford University Press (2020).

DOI: 10.1093/oso/9780190067717.001.0001

A representative system can thus seem legally authorized when in fact it only codifies a social partition of the human community that preceded it. The initial establishment of a system of representation "entail[s] drawing a frontier between 'us' and 'them,' those who belong to the 'demos' and those who are outside it."[2] The word *frontier* might suggest that the boundaries are always spatial in nature, but of course, this is not the case. The American Revolution established boundaries both between the United States and England and, simultaneously, between the white men who were eligible to vote in the new state and the women, African Americans, and Native Americans who were not, despite residing within its borders.

Once the boundaries of an electorate are set, its decisions may seem to meet our tests of democratic legitimacy, but such communities are democratic only from the perspective of those who have perpetrated, or at least have benefited from, an act that itself can be neither legal nor justified. In sum, even polities formally structured by equality and law seem inevitably to rest on exclusion and arbitrariness.

The effects of this extra-legal division are debatable, but no theorist calls attention to this phenomenon in order to praise it. To Giorgio Agamben, for example, this flawed foundation is the source, among other things, of extravagant claims of executive power in times of crisis.[3] To Robert Cover, it is a reminder of the precariously close, and indeed tragic, relation between law and violence.[4] To Bonnie Honig, it is the cause of the ambivalent and often hostile relationship between democracies and foreigners.[5] And to Carl Schmitt, the general author of this line of thought, it is all we need to know in order to understand that representative parliamentary democracy is a self-deluding sham that must ultimately rely on, or give way to, a regime with decisionistic authority.[6] In general, we can say that the problem posed is whether any representative, democratic regime can really claim legitimacy under the principles that purport to structure its ordinary practice. What, if anything, could render acceptable the existence of representation founded on a primordial, undemocratic exclusion?

Although it has long been recognized that the western genre of film often traffics in questions of the relation between violence and the law, and although there has also been some critical attention recently to John Ford's *The Man Who Shot Liberty Valance* (1962),[7] it has not been generally recognized that the film examines precisely this democratic paradox through a parable of state formation and representative choice set in the pre-industrial American West. I maintain that *Liberty Valance* not only succeeds in representing the dilemma—which would be enough of an achievement for a two-hour film that is also fairly entertaining—but actually suggests a novel response to this significant problem at the core of democratic theory.

At the heart of the film is a model of both how a representative might be chosen from a people that is yet inchoate as well as an examination of the burdens that such a representative might bear. Without giving too much away at this point, we can say that this model has something to do with relating both law and power to time and narrative. While there is no suggestion that a democratic community can have an origin apart from violence and exclusion, there is a possibility that violence and exclusion might be less than arbitrary and, in some sense, tolerable, at least to the point where it might be possible to publically acknowledge and thus take and bear responsibility for it. But the costs of this resolution, at least to democracy's self-image and its representatives, remain high.

Much of the literature on the democratic paradox, as Honig points out, attempts to elide its fundamentally political character by transforming it into a manageable problem of justification, "a problem that rules might solve."[8] She proposes instead that we embrace "the fecundity of undecidability, a trait that suggests that our cherished ideals—law, the people, general will, deliberation—are implicated in that to which deliberative democratic theory opposes them: violence, multitude, the will of all, decision."[9] Sensitive, as few others are, to the complicated intertwining of the forces inside and outside of the law, she bravely suggests that we remain "squarely in the paradox of politics—that irresolvable and productive paradox in which a future is claimed on behalf of peoples and rights that are not yet and may never be."[10]

While this proposal is a great improvement on previous formulations, it relies on an avowed will to regard the situation with "a sense of optimism and possibility."[11] Although Honig's optimism is not the vision of historical progress that democrats like Immanuel Kant and Jürgen Habermas rely on, it traces too lightly, I fear, over the issues of violence and exclusion that *Liberty Valance* throws into sharp relief. The differences between the state and the unformed multitude may well be a source of creativity, but it is a paramount political problem that they are also a source of danger. If Schmitt was wrong that the only solution was for a state to be "homogeneous" (a mistake based in his own sort of optimism about the power of decision), he was certainly right about the stakes of the question: so long as we have states and representative governments, we will have exclusion and antagonism, not just originally but continuously.

In *Liberty Valance,* I suggest, we have, along with a sober acknowledgment of this fact, a perspective that suggests how we might approach the democratic paradox and acknowledge the arbitrariness at the heart of our democracy without allowing it to completely dissolve our sense of the authority of law or of the tolerability of democratic representation. In place of optimism, I see in the film a pessimism that views representation as a necessary burden that allows us to carry on with democracy while exacting a high price to our happiness for doing so. It is a familiar observation about film that its representation rests on the exclusion symbolized by the screen-frame—that is to say, any shot enforces the absence of whatever is outside the four sides of the rectangle. *Liberty Valance* makes the same process visible in politics, even in the most democratic setting. Yet it does not repudiate democratic representation; it is just honest about the costs as it reformulates its legitimacy.

FACT, LEGEND, AND STORY

Ford's movie was derived from an eponymous short story by Dorothy Johnson, who also wrote "A Man Called Horse" and "The Hanging Tree," which were filmed by other directors. In the story, the title already has the curious double meaning that is the key both to the plot and to our paradox: one man shoots the dangerous, improbably named bandit Liberty Valance, but another acquires the reputation for having done so. One of these men (in the movie, Jimmy Stewart as Ransom Stoddard) becomes the representative of the community as it transitions from an inchoate state of nature to a modern, democratic state, while the other (John Wayne as Tom Doniphon) fades into obscurity. The cooperation and tension between these two, and their rivalry for the same woman (Vera Miles as Hallie Ericsson), drives Johnson's story, which is told very briefly in prose so spare it is almost telegraphic.[12] But in the film, which is far more discursive and adds many characters and settings, another layer of meaning is added to the title: a third "shooter." For as someone who has taken an existing story and put it on film, John Ford has "shot" Liberty Valance in the cinematic sense.[13] In the process, he turns a pithy, interesting, psychological tale into a parable for the formation of a country and a representation of democratic representation in its elemental essence.

Robert Pippin briefly notes this sense of Ford as a third shooter in his illuminating lecture on the film.[14] However, he does not accord it much significance. To Pippin, the film is "at its core a tragedy, a mythically significant or representative tragedy,"[15] and on this interpretation, the main tragic figure is Doniphon, the Wayne character, who is repaid for his nobility by having everything taken away from him and being forgotten. But while Doniphon is certainly a tragic figure, and while Pippin is careful to notice many important features of the film that have not been appreciated before, I think he is misled here by his book's focus on three films in which John Wayne is a lead actor. The moniker "The Man Who Shot Liberty Valance" refers to (at least) two men—Doniphon and Stoddard—and the film is equally about both them and the state that they make, and could only make, together with Hallie.

Unlike Johnson's story, the film chronicles the transition that a community endures from an anarchic (though often cooperative) state of nature, where law is ineffective, to a sovereign legal state with democratic representation, where individuals can no longer use force independently. What happens to Doniphon is part of the price to be paid for that transition, and if we are meant to be reminded of that price, we are also meant to recognize the transition as a human achievement.[16]

To call the film a tragedy makes it Doniphon's story when in fact it is the story of a would-be democratic society and its enemy, unbounded Liberty.[17] Generally speaking, the central character of a story is the one who undergoes some kind of change. By that measure (as we shall see), Stoddard is at the narrative's core. But more important than any of the several characters is the change, through their interaction, of the community itself. It is this social and political change—the demise of lawless Liberty and the securing of statehood and representation—that alters the fates of the characters, none of whom embodies this state as a whole. That law and liberty are originally enemies is the uncomfortable truth that *Liberty Valance* forces us to confront (as Hobbes, in his own way, did as well). Though the film is not a tragedy, I argue it is pessimistic in the sense that it refuses the familiar narrative of democratic progress, where civic freedom produces widespread happiness. Each of the three main characters pays a distinct price for the existence of the state they help bring about, with Hallie's perhaps the most distinct of all.

The film's best-known line ("print the legend") in fact represents something like the opposite of its perspective[18]—which is to carefully deconstruct and reveal (without debunking) the complicated interrelation of law and power in the formation of any state. In the story, both of these forces are depicted as incapable, by themselves, of creating or sustaining order in something that resembles a state of nature. But for violence to be exercised on behalf of law, it is not enough that it be principled or just—Doniphon is both of these things already (i.e., principled and violent), but he is also thoroughly uninterested in governing his fellow citizens, even if they would elect him. Rather, it is only when he is affectively engaged (by love) that he comes to the aid of law and legality, and he does so knowing that he will not benefit from his engagement. That is to say, the violence he ultimately performs is not (or not only) an act of domination but also (and even principally) an act of self-sacrifice. Indeed, he does not "collect" on his violence. Instead, his actions are hidden behind the figure of another's authorship, and he is forgotten.

Likewise, "law," as initially embodied in Stoddard, is ineffectual and abstract when it attempts to act on its own. It is also uncommitted. Ransom Stoddard has the option (we are constantly reminded) of leaving the town where the action takes place rather than remaining to solve its problems. It is an option he is often tempted by, and like Doniphon, his steadfastness turns out not to be supported by a disinterested devotion to justice but by an erotic tie that is stronger than any calculation of interest or legality. And he too fails to benefit from the institution of justice in the way he optimistically expects at the beginning.

Hallie, whose place in the film is complex, seemingly gets what she and the other ordinary citizens want: to live in a law-abiding community and to witness its material development. And yet most viewers of the film get the distinct impression that she does not enjoy the result as we, or she, might have expected. This is in part because she retains erotic ties to both men and thus shares in the suffering of both, but also, as I explore later, because the gendered aspects of their relationships impose special burdens on her that the others do not share.

As we will see, "the man who shot Liberty Valance"—the representative and lawgiver who instantiates a legal order where there was none—is really *both* Wayne and Stewart, neither one of them being sufficient to the task by themselves and both needing and acknowledging the other in the process of state formation. And yet the film itself, in revealing what it takes to have been hidden, is hardly intended as an unpatriotic act. On the contrary, we are meant to be strengthened, if sobered, by the revelation that law is not self-generating or self-sustaining but requires a sacrifice to succeed.

Precisely by printing (or shooting) the facts alongside the legend, the filmmaker, it will transpire, perpetuates the fortuitous moment of state formation.[19] What constitutes the state, then, is neither law nor power by themselves, but rather *the matrix of representation*, made from eros and narrative, that creates the relationship between them—here, a film, but perhaps more generally, a sustaining narrative. It is this matrix, I say, that constitutes a response to the democratic paradox—not a *resolution* of it certainly, but a response that renders it less crippling. This response also reveals how inheritors of such moments remain both responsible for and implicated in the sustaining of modern states. Let us see how this happens.

WESTERN LAW, EASTERN PROMISES

The story opens with the return (by steam train) of Senator Ransom Stoddard and his wife Hallie to the town of Shinbone in an unnamed western state.[20] The arrival of the Senator is a big story to the local newspaper editor. And when he learns that the Senator has returned for the funeral of an unknown man, he demands to know the reason. In Dorothy Johnson's story, the Senator considers the matter but then demurs, giving the bland answer that the deceased was an old friend. The first signal that the film will be different from the short story—a public rather than a private matter—is that the Senator, after consulting with Hallie, admits the editor's claim ("I have a right to the story." "Yes, I suppose you have."). The story we are to witness has been hidden for decades. At the end of the film, we will learn, it remains hidden (except, of course, to us)—the editor declines to publish what he learned. So the audience is, in effect, the secret spectator for a secret tale of (what turns out to be) state (pro)creation. The film leaves each viewer in the position of the editor, with a choice to make about whether to acknowledge the past and, if so, in what way.

After the Senator agrees to tell his story, the film in effect commences for a second time. A flashback begins that will not end until the final minutes of the film. Stoddard is seen venturing into the territory by stagecoach (thirty or more years earlier) when his party is assaulted by Liberty Valance (Lee Marvin), who leads a team of well-armed bandits. After surviving the robbery, Stoddard establishes himself in Shinbone, first by washing dishes at a restaurant run by Swedish immigrants. Their daughter Hallie is planning to marry Doniphon, but she is attracted to Stoddard's learning and eastern sophistication. Stoddard opens a school and, eventually, becomes a town leader. The members of the town want the territory to become a state, but Valance, paid by the ranchers who oppose statehood, continues to terrorize them. After several confrontations, Stoddard appears to kill Valance in a shoot-out, marries Hallie, and later becomes the first state governor. But in fact it was Doniphon who killed Valance, shooting from where he could not be seen. And though the town eventually forgets about Doniphon entirely, Ransom and Hallie cannot help but return to his funeral.

Having sketched the plot in outline, I now focus on some specific scenes that reveal the film's perspective on representation and state formation and the erotic dynamics between Ransom, Doniphon, and Hallie that underlie them (leaving many other interesting themes to one side).

The contrast between civil society and the dangerous space of untamed Liberty is established early on, when Valance robs the travelers more violently than he needs to. Ransom protests, asserting his standing as a lawyer, and Valence beats him and then mocks him. When Stoddard's law books are discovered in the luggage, Valence takes malicious pleasure in tearing them up and then, uttering the words "I'll teach you law! Western law!" proceeds to beat Ransom further with a silver-handled whip (his trademark weapon). Valance is only prevented from killing Stoddard when one of his own men restrains him. Liberty, we are meant to understand, loathes the "eastern" written law or any kind of restraint to his behavior. Indeed, his cruelty is most provoked not by a desire for money or personal authority (he has plenty of one and doesn't care for the other) but precisely by any attempt to regulate or civilize him.[21] Though we later learn that he is in the pay of the cattle barons, it is clear that he despises the (would-be) law-abiding townspeople anyway and is a danger to all even when he acts on his own, which he often does.

The contrast between Liberty's grandiose self-licensing and Stoddard's status as an effete law-bearer (literally carrying the books of law from the east to the west)[22] is immediately complicated, however, by the arrival of Doniphon. Left for dead in the desert, Stoddard is rescued by Doniphon, who brings him into town and into the care of Hallie. Somewhat improbably, Stoddard and Doniphon almost immediately fall into a conversation about the nature of law. Stoddard wants Liberty Valance arrested. Doniphon says, "I know those law books mean a lot to you. But not out here. Out here a man settles his own problems," and slaps his pistol for emphasis. Stoddard replies, "Do you know what you're saying to me? You're saying just exactly what Liberty Valance said."

In one sense, Doniphon is nothing like Liberty; he has just rescued Stoddard from the desert where Liberty abandoned him. But of course, Stoddard's concern is that Doniphon is endorsing the "western law" Liberty was referring to, even if he would never enforce it as viciously. Doniphon does share Valance's contempt for organized authority: the scene ends with Doniphon conspicuously mocking the town's ineffectual marshal—taking his hat off of his head and dropping it on the floor while knowing the marshal will do nothing in return.

But then why does Doniphon, well-known to be more than a match for Liberty, tolerate his continued dangerous presence?[23] Pippin supplies a plausible answer: it is, he argues "precisely *because* [Doniphon] feels so self-sufficient and independent that he sees no need" to confront Valance.[24] We could add to this that, so long as he doesn't threaten Doniphon, there is something convenient for him in having Liberty around. Doniphon's reputation as a tough guy benefits from the rivalry and the comparison. And there is the affinity that Stoddard has already put his finger on.

To all this, however, we must add something else. If Doniphon were to dispose of Liberty on behalf of the town, he would be taking it under his protection, putting it under his own rule. And this is a responsibility he has no desire for. He wishes the town well, but he has no inclination to care for it or to govern it. The town's dilemma is thus indeed Hobbesian: either the powerful wish to dominate, or if they do not, they are self-sufficient and have no reason or desire to help. Yet without such help, Ransom's project of democracy and democratic law cannot get off the ground, as he soon discovers. Stoddard wants to bring democratic law to the town but lacks the power to defeat law's enemies; Doniphon has the power but not the interest. What is it that combines law and power? And can they combine in some way that is not arbitrary or despotic?

To answer this question, we must consider their relations both with and through Hallie, who (although her position is unique) articulates the active desires of the *demos*. She is not (as she might be in other films) a token passed between the two men but a live participant in a three-pointed relationship that endures even after her ultimate marriage to Stoddard. The success of that relationship requires a delicate reciprocity that does not come naturally to any of the characters. After his humiliation by Valance, the film puts Stoddard in an apron and displays his physical vulnerability at the hands of Liberty, while Doniphon, in his ten-gallon hat, is immune and independent. Their mutual affection for Hallie seems bound to lead to conflict. But a series of failed attempts at getting along pave the way for a transformation that is equally erotic and political.

EQUALITY AND ITS ABSENCES

Ford goes out of his way to emphasize visually the multiethnic character of Shinbone, a diversity that forms no part of Johnson's original story and that seems to add little to the plot of the film, but in fact adds a great deal when we consider the film as a parable of the representative condition. On repeated viewing, the contrast between the visual diversity and the monochromatic screenplay is one of the most striking elements of the film. One of the first shots of the old town of Shinbone focuses on the "Cantina" where Mexicans (i.e., Mexican Americans) lounge outside in large sombreros for us to notice. Throughout the film, there are many moments when we hear the music from the Cantina and the camera will notice the Mexican Americans, even if the main speaking characters do not. It even turns out that the town marshal, Link Appleyard, has a large Spanish-speaking family. Again, these Latinos have no particular role to play in the main action of the film; the original story includes no one but whites—so why include them at all?[25]

A similar question can be asked about one of the most prominent speaking characters added to the story by the screenwriters: Pompey (Woody Strode), Tom Doniphon's African American ranch hand who has the name of a Roman Republican hero.[26] His race is hardly mentioned at all in the script, but his second-class status is indicated by a variety of visual cues, including his physical exclusion, clearly noted, from the social and political gatherings of whites. Again, nothing in the overall plot seems to require the role of Pompey to be portrayed by a black actor. All of the other ranch hands seen in the film are white. So what is the point of casting a black actor in the role and then making that fact nearly unspeakable?

The answer to these questions, I think, is to be found in the intricate scene that comes at the very center of the movie, where the gap between words and their enactment—and between a population and their representative—is vividly rendered. Ransom has settled into town and, in addition to his fledging law practice, has begun a school. Hallie was his first student, but as there is no other school in town and even many of the adults (like Doniphon) are functionally illiterate, he has a highly varied classroom. When Stoddard enters the room, we see the entire group framed together in tableau, and they are young and old, immigrant and native, black and white and brown. In fact, it is a group of people much more likely to be representative of, say, a Los Angeles street corner in 1962 than the classroom of a small farming town in a western territory during the 1870s. Given that the United States was in the midst of the conflicts about the racial integration of its schools at the time of the film's making, the tableau seems designed to send a powerful message.[27] It communicates the diversity of the actual population of Shinbone, which stands in here for the United States as a whole, and the question of whether that whole will be represented in the state to be made.

The message, however, is as much about the obstacles to equality and inclusion as it is a vision of their enactment. The symbolic elements in this scene are so many, and so complicated, that it is difficult to convey their combined effect. But the gathering of races, sexes, and ages tells us that this is no ordinary classroom. The blackboard is already inscribed with the motto that ties the schoolroom to Ransom's status as a law-bearer, "Education is the basis of law and order"—a very dubious claim, from the standpoint of what we have seen thus far. Significantly, the words will later be erased.

The lesson of the day is also most unusual, even surreal. Ransom begins by "reviewing" (supposedly for the new students) the nature of democracy. He calls upon Hallie's mother Nora, who begins hesitantly, but with increasing confidence, in noticeably accented English: "The United States is a republic. And a republic is a state in which the people are the boss!" Then, there begins a very strange exchange between Ransom and Pompey, who, we will later learn, is there as a student against Doniphon's wishes:

RANSOM: Now I wonder if anyone in class remembers what the basic law of the land is called? Now you remember that I told you it had to be added to and changed from time to time by things called 'amendments'. Now does anyone remember? . . . Julietta, your hand's always up. Here. Let's . . . Pompey, you try this one.

POMPEY: It was writ' by Mr. Thomas Jefferson of Virginia.

RANSOM: Was "written," Pompey.

POMPEY: Written by Mr. Thomas Jefferson. And he called it the Constitution.

RANSOM: Declaration of Independence.

POMPEY: Uh, it begun with the words, uh, we hold these truths to be, uh . . .

CHARLIE (an adult, white ranch hand): [whispering] Self-evident!

RANSOM: Let him alone, Charlie.

POMPEY: Self-evident, that, uh . . .

RANSOM: That all men are created equal. . . . That's fine, Pompey.

POMPEY: I knew that, Mr. Ranse, but I just plum forgot it.

RANSOM: Oh, that's alright, Pompey. A lot of people forget that part of it.

Throughout this part of the scene, Stoddard appears patronizing, and the exchange clearly establishes a hierarchy between teacher and student. But given the subject, that can hardly be the whole point. In the first place, Ransom, from his description, has in fact asked Pompey to name the Constitution, but when Pompey describes Thomas Jefferson as its sole author, Ransom only corrects his grammar. Then, when Pompey *does* name the Constitution, Ransom says "Declaration of Independence" as though it is a correction, when in fact Pompey has given the correct answer to his initial question. And finally, when Pompey begins to recite the second (not the first) paragraph of the Declaration, Ransom leaves that uncorrected until Pompey needs his help with the crucial words—words that are belied by the multiple hierarchies in which the conversation partners are embedded.

What has happened here? For one thing, it has been implied that the Declaration and its sovereign grant of equality, not the Constitution, is the "basic law" of the United States. For another, it has been established that this fundamental fact is hard to remember, even among those for whom it is most important to remember, despite its supposed "self-evident" nature. And one might also conclude that Stoddard, though he has opened his classroom to all, still condescends to his students rather than serving them, and perhaps does not treat them as equals to one another or himself.

In other words, just as the egalitarian screenplay is supplemented by a visual depiction that shows something more racially and sexually hierarchical, here it is practically spelled out for us how the text of the Declaration is only enacted and meaningful (to the extent that it is meaningful) in a setting where race and sex have an unspoken power. Yet though Stoddard is the teacher, Pompey does not quite answer the question he has been asked. And while Pompey needs help in completing the answer, the answer he gives to the question of "fundamental law" is in fact better and more important then the "correct" answer would have been.[28]

What does this mean? For a movie released at the height of the civil rights movement, I don't think it is too much of a stretch to say that what we have here is an image of a variegated community groping awkwardly, and with missteps, toward a foundational memory that is obscured and yet determining (much like the story of the film itself). In other words, we have a kind of parable within the parable that lets us know some implications of the larger story the movie cannot explicitly address. The law that Ransom seeks to instantiate (and that Ford is attempting to buttress) is a law of equality, the implications of which, even in 1962, are far from fully materialized. And Stoddard's air of superiority notwithstanding, the images show us that no race has a monopoly on this law's meaning. The classroom, remarkably, represents both equality and its absence—and the divisions of race (and of gender and ethnicity) that are responsible for that absence.[29] It shows the possibilities, and the limits, of what the law-bearer can accomplish on his own.

Stoddard, at this point in the film, is a lawyer and a teacher, but *he is not yet a representative* or, I think, even a proper citizen of Shinbone. He speaks to his charges from the outside, as a tutor, rather than from the inside, as a representative would.

Those limits are made even more clear when the lesson, hardly begun, is interrupted by the return of Doniphon, who has been away on business. He roughly tells both Pompey and Hallie that they have no business in school (Hallie resists; Pompey does not). More importantly, though, he announces the impending return of Liberty Valance, who, along with other thugs, plans to prevent the town from electing pro-statehood delegates to an impending territorial convention. "Votes," he says, as if he had heard the lesson and was now refuting it, "won't stand up against guns." Doniphon and Ransom argue with the painted American flag between them. Ransom calls off class, sadly erases his slogan and, when Hallie protests, says, "When force threatens, talk's no good anymore."

The school breaks up in disarray. The point has been made: when Doniphon and Ransom are at odds, the democratic project is in danger. The former aims only to defend himself and advises the townspeople, for their own safety, to abandon their drive for statehood. Ransom no longer wears an apron, but he has no answer to Valance's threat. Hallie attempts to mediate between them but fails.

THE EROTIC BINDING OF THE FORCE OF LAW

After this failure, the film shows the sovereign state and a representative relationship made, in effect, twice: the first time as farce and the second as tragedy. That is, there are two scenes in which we see, as clearly as it is possible to see, the sovereignty of a legal community established over a violent opposition and the selection of a representative to speak for that community. In both scenes, Liberty Valance is defeated: in the first, he is defeated democratically and ineffectually—he is outvoted but undeterred; in the second, he is killed and his threat to civil society permanently ended. The doubling is necessary to bring home the point, among others, that it is not enough for those who oppose the state to be outvoted when their antagonism amounts to existential opposition. But the doubling also emphasizes the insufficiency of both law and violence, acting separately, to establish the identity and sovereignty of the *demos*. This is the path, I maintain, between the legends of liberalism and the "facts" of decisionism, as it were, that the film's narrative means to thread us through. The difference between the two scenes is Hallie; it is her action and choice that sets in motion the genuinely effective state-making. She also creates the erotic tie that binds Ransom to the community and to his duty as a representative.

Some time after the schoolroom scene, a meeting of the townspeople is convened for the purpose of electing two delegates to the territorial convention. The scene Ford shows us is again so rife with significant images that it is difficult to recognize them all on first viewing. Pompey, his supposed equality once again forgotten, sits motionless and wordless, cradling his rifle, outside the meeting hall as the town's white men come to the front door and, being recognized by name, are allowed to enter. (In fact, he is guarding the meeting, but that only becomes apparent later, when it is threatened by Liberty.) Despite the orderly procession into the meeting, however, there is chaos inside. There is no chair or order of business. The citizens talk and shout at one another—not in a violent way, but in a way that shows the utter lack of organization or hierarchy among them. How can the meeting come to order if there are no rules or convener? But how can there be a convener if there has been no previous meeting to appoint one? The infinite regress of democratic authority is both audible and visible. The paradox of democratic founding is on clear display.

In the midst of the noise, Stoddard sits silently, looking depressed, just one citizen among many. Doniphon sits on the bar, looking amused at what is going on around and beneath him. Finally, after a while, he climbs down off the bar, picks up a giant mallet (a "bung-starter," in fact, used to open beer kegs) and hammers an unoccupied table at the front of the room, calling the meeting to order. All fall silent. Doniphon immediately nominates Stoddard to conduct the meeting. The motion is met with acclaim. As Stoddard comes to the front, Doniphon tosses him the mallet and says, "There's your regulator, pilgrim." So authorized, Stoddard goes on to conduct the meeting.

For a moment, it seems like law and force can work together easily and harmoniously. Doniphon has stilled the chaos and then graciously turned the proceedings over to someone who will conduct them fairly and according to law. One might even expect Doniphon and Stoddard to be elected as the two delegates. But that is not what happens. After giving an impassioned, optimistic speech on behalf of statehood ("We want statehood! . . . It means progress for the future!"), Stoddard nominates Doniphon as a delegate. But Doniphon refuses: he grabs the mallet, says that he's got "personal plans" (his planned marriage to Hallie) that prevent his service, and then hands the mallet back to Stoddard and tells him to go on.

At this point, Liberty Valance rides up and approaches the doorway of the meeting. The doorkeepers attempt to refuse him entrance, saying he doesn't live in the district. Liberty replies, "I live where I hang my hat," and bursts into the room through swinging doors that form the highly permeable boundary to the political space of the meeting.

This exchange is important because it highlights the central problem the townspeople face, one that Doniphon cannot solve: until their sovereignty and borders are secure, they cannot exclude anyone who claims to be a member of their community, no matter how inimical or hostile his presence is to the community itself. In fact, it is not clear that Liberty lives anywhere in particular—we never see his residence—but then why should he? Part of his role as an embodiment of natural freedom is that he can go anywhere, whenever he likes, without having to ask anyone's permission. There being no state, there can be no hard boundaries or law of citizenship. Inside the meeting, though no one agrees with Valance, no one can deny his right to be present either, even if Stoddard pointedly lists his domicile as "address unknown."

Valance has one of his lackeys nominate him and threatens all those present that there will be unpleasant consequences if he is not elected. But the townspeople, secure in Doniphon's presence, nominate Stoddard and the town's newspaper editor as delegates. When the time for voting comes, Valance strides to the front of the room and repeats his threats. When his name is called, he raises his silver whip (in a nice bit of symbolism) to vote for himself, but except for his two lackeys, the room is motionless. For the only time in the film before his death, Valance is silent and looks uncertain how to proceed. Stoddard and the editor are acclaimed as the delegates by the others. Doniphon declares that the election is over and the bar is open, and the citizens revert to the boisterous chaos that preceded the meeting. But Valance tells Stoddard plainly not only that the election is meaningless but that he will kill him that night if he doesn't leave town.

Once again, Doniphon and Stoddard's efforts to work together have failed, or have only partially succeeded. They have won the election but still are not truly united; rather, they have followed one another serially. Civil society needs boundaries and a rule of membership—here to exclude those who would threaten its democratic character—but neither man has succeeded in sustaining them. The election, and Stoddard's status as a representative, will be trumped by violence, and the fledgling state will be disbanded. At this point, neither man sees an alternative to this outcome. For either Ransom or Doniphon to kill Valance would violate his principles (for Ransom, the principle of acting through law; for Tom, the principle to only act in self-defense), but without the death of Liberty, the project of sovereign law will fail.

In the crucial scene that follows, the dark double of the first, Ransom faces up to Liberty on a nighttime street. This time, Ransom is alone (or appears to be). He has a gun but, since he hardly knows how to use it, believes he has no chance. Just as Liberty's powers were no powers at all in the meeting room and he was rendered speechless, so here Ransom (in an apron again) is isolated and mute. He makes no speeches. Liberty mocks him and shoots the gun out of his right hand, forcing him to pick it up with his left. Then, they fire at the same time, and miraculously, Liberty falls dead and Ransom escapes further injury. Now the threat of Valance has finally been removed, the sovereign monopoly on the use of force has been established. Ransom begins his career as "the man who shot Liberty Valance" and as a representative for Shinbone and, eventually, the entire state.

All is not as it seems, however. This scene, already a double, itself has a double. We will see the same scene over again, later in the film (a flashback within the flashback) from a different perspective, when Doniphon informs Stoddard that he was not, after all, alone in the street. Doniphon, hidden in a dark alley, firing at the same time as the other two but unseen and unheard, is the true killer of Liberty Valance. Both men, it turns out, have violated their principles, Stoddard by picking up a gun outside of the law and Doniphon by ambushing someone who was not threatening him. But their twin actions solve the problem laid out in the previous scene. Stoddard has appeared to defend himself and, thereby, the legal regime he has helped to bring about. The threat of Liberty has been eliminated, and the talents of Stoddard and Doniphon have been combined into a single representative figure—"the man who shot Liberty Valance"—a self-executing law and a self-sustaining sovereign who now, with the face of Ransom, can continue the project of statehood.

Why have they each done what they were resolved not to do? The answer is the same for both—they love Hallie, and between the election and the shoot-out, they have each been reminded of what this requires by Hallie herself. Ransom has realized that he cannot bear to leave Hallie, or the town, even at the cost of his own life. And Tom, knowing that Hallie does not want Ransom to die, does for her what he would not do for himself. But Ransom and Tom do not merely *cooperate*; rather, they are *united* by eros into a new identity that can only exist as a narrative artifact. What kind of man is "The Man Who Shot Liberty Valance"?

THE EROTIC CONTRACT

There can be little doubt that the social union brought into being by the end of the film is both stabilized and symbolized by the marital tie between Ransom and Hallie. Equally, one could track the plot of the film as Ransom's progress from ineffectual, feminized kitchen help to authoritative, masculine politician. We could, in other words, take the film to simply affirm heterosexual marriage (and the gender subordination it entails) as a central element of the sovereign state of law: "civil freedom," as Carole

Pateman put it, grounded "upon patriarchal right."[30] If this were the sum total of the film's sexual politics, then it would resemble that of many other films, and we would have to conclude that, however novel its approach to sovereignty was in some respects, in this it simply repeats (and relies on) traditional sex roles. But "The Man Who Shot Liberty Valance" is not Ransom alone.

Though the film confirms gender conventions (as it confirms a conventional state), the erotic relations depicted within it are hardly ordinary. Doniphon and Stoddard each have a relationship with Hallie *and through her with one another*. Theirs is a peculiarly triangular arrangement not at all captured by the idea of sexual rivalry. Despite Ransom's marriage to Hallie, Doniphon never disappears from their relationship. The whole frame of the movie—the return of Ransom and Hallie to pay tribute to Doniphon—makes that unmistakable. And Ransom's political name shows how much he owes his identity to Doniphon. The marriage of Ransom and Hallie may (and must) appear conventional, but Doniphon's continuous presence in their relationship is one of the secrets that we, as citizens, are brought to understand by the film's revelations.

What, then, is the nature of their bond, such that it can be both erotic and political? Both feminism and queer theory have developed a language to think about this kind of relationship. Eve Kosofsky Sedgwick's question of *Billy Budd*—"What are the operations necessary to deploy male-male desire as the glue rather than as the solvent of a hierarchical male disciplinary order?"—seems to be exactly the one that the film is attempting to answer. From this perspective, Stoddard's growth in masculinity over the course of the film appears as an apprenticeship to Doniphon, culminating in a homosocial bond "routed through triangular relations involving a woman."[31] Liberty Valance is the man who must be killed precisely because he routinely feminizes Stoddard and others. Ransom's induction into the masculine order conforms to the model laid out by Pierre Bourdieu: "manliness," he says, "is an eminently *relational* notion, constructed in front of and for other men and against femininity, in a kind of *fear* of the female, firstly in oneself."[32] Stoddard emulates Doniphon and Doniphon, in his own way, emulates Stoddard (becoming part of his project of law), and all for the sake of Hallie, but not because they fear her. Rather, they exorcise their own femininity by together combating an emasculating Liberty in her name.

While this reading gets us closer to the truth, it too has the effect of reducing Hallie to an audience, and a token, when she is clearly something more. To render the three as equally important (though certainly not equal in other respects), I suggest thinking of their bond as an erotic one, as Anne Carson has defined eros: "where eros is lack, its activation calls for three structural components—lover, beloved, and that which comes between them. They are three points of transformation on a circuit of possible relationship, electrified by desire so that they touch not touching. Conjoined they are held apart."[33] For these three characters, their relations with each of the others is both enabled and obstructed by the presence of the third. This is even true for Ransom and Hallie following their marriage. As many viewers have noticed, they have no children, and they do not, in their return to Shinbone, seem very affectionate. In fact; in the whole movie, we never see them kiss. Although they are together, it is as if the presence of Doniphon continuously interrupts their union (while also preserving it).

Eros, not contract or violence, is the force that binds all three together (and yet apart)—and through them, the community—with a power that is all the stronger for being unconsummated. In one of the final scenes of the film, Hallie has brought a cactus rose in from the desert and placed it on Tom's coffin.[34] Some have interpreted this to mean that she "really" loves Tom (as opposed to Ransom) and always has. But this makes no sense—she was never under any obligation to leave Tom and clearly chose to do so. What does make sense, and is merely hard to acknowledge, is that she loved them both—bigamously, one could say—and would perhaps have continued to do so outwardly if the rules of society permitted. Or perhaps it is best to say that Hallie, like the rest of the community she often speaks for, loves "The Man Who Shot Liberty Valance"—the composite representative created by the erotic bond. And unlike the rest of the community (but like us), she knows his two faces, the fact and the legend.[35] By continuing to care for both, she maintains the bond of identity between them to the end.

In both politics and cinema, it can be easy to see eros as a destructive force (the *femme fatale*, the sex scandal), one that primarily instigates conflict. Or if it is to be constructive, it is supposed to work through conventional forms, like heterosexual marriage. What is so unusual in this film is the way in which an erotic rivalry becomes a form of cooperation so that power and law enlist one another's support against a chaos that is destructive and sadistic. The rivalry is not resolved with a victory for one party but rather crystallized in a continuing relationship that preserves the foundational moment.

More importantly, however, I believe this presentation of eros transforms our perception of "power" and "law" so that they do not appear to be opposite forms of social organization. Our approach to the paradox at the foundation of democracy cannot be to find a magical (or miraculous) ground to pre-authorize foundational arbitrary power, nor can it be to discover some perfectly self-authorizing law or rational procedure. Rather, only when we see law and power not as originary and *opposite* forces but as two halves of an erotic whole can we understand the formation of a state as an act worth remembering and acknowledging, with all attendant costs and sacrifices. It would be wrong, then, to see the characters as "symbols"—as if ideas like "law" and "power" were *normally* disembodied phenomena that a work of fiction might choose to represent as human. The point is rather that in politics, ideas and power can only exist as the expression of embodied beings who can always, in principle, relate to one another erotically.

Especially in the literature derived from Carl Schmitt, discourse on the democratic paradox can operate within the grip of a political ontology in which law and power are treated like matter and anti-matter—as if they naturally operate in wholly separate registers (law within a state; power outside) and must annihilate one another whenever they meet. From this perspective, any relationship between them naturally looks paradoxical or self-contradictory, or as if one is simply in service to the other. By contrast, when we understand both as human activities, performed by individuals whose potentials exist within a shared horizon of narrative meaning, we are better positioned to articulate and grasp how the democratic political origin of sovereign authority might be theorized.

I do not mean, of course, that the bond of eros (much less the modern state) and the representative system it engenders is something we can uncritically celebrate in any form. Even though the three characters here have equal stature in some sense, their roles remain gender-delimited, where men "belong on the side of all things external, official, public, straight, high . . . [and] perform all the brief, dangerous, and spectacular acts."[36] Though Hallie participates emotionally in the forging of the erotico-political union, she never participates politically in the ordinary sense, and there is no forum for her to do so. (Whether a refashioned erotic bond could perform the same function of political adhesion while providing for more genuine equality is not something I can answer here.)

But my question has not been whether a representative sovereign democracy can be *celebrated* but whether it can be *tolerated*. Even without calling attention to the gender prescriptions embedded within it, the erotic contract that *Liberty Valance* imagines will inevitably be, as in Carson's sapphic interpretation, bittersweet. Eros is always a particular attraction; it unites two or several but never all because it also excludes as it unites. Yet what it unites, it unites humanistically—like Rousseau's fictitious Lawgiver, it persuades without convincing and forces without violence, which is to say it shows how reason and power can be complementary elements of political attachment, and not always (or only) rival sources of social organization.

From one perspective, of course, it is difficult to think of the state as grounded in an erotic contract—we cannot possibly know or care about all of our fellow citizens as deeply or intimately as a love-partner. On the other hand, it is not wrong to believe that our commitment to our fellow citizens is something more than a rational calculation, an agreement to a set of principles, or the worship of an abstraction. Our commitment to preserving their humanity is grounded in the project of mutual humanization that we continuously participate in, which is clearly a project with an erotic dimension. The lack of consummation actually *preserves* that connection here and, in so doing, shows how it may be spread beyond intimate couples.

THE STATE'S RANSOM

Many interpretations of the film, including those of Robert Pippin and Tag Gallagher, are hostile to the character of Ransom Stoddard. A "ransom" is supposed to be something one pays to go free, yet it seems to them that Stoddard has not paid at all but rather benefitted from his part in the story while the full expense is left to Doniphon. To them, Stoddard even seems to be patronizing and unappreciative.[37] Why, then, is Ransom named Ransom? What price has he paid?

The answer, I believe, can be found in the last scenes of the flashback. Having recovered from his duel, Stoddard travels to "Capitol City" as one of Shinbone's representatives to the territorial convention that will in turn send a representative to Washington to argue for (or against) statehood. Some commentators have seen this scene as extraneous, but I think it is essential to understanding the burden that Ransom shares, as the people's representative, along with his rewards. At the convention, the ranchers (who oppose statehood) nominate someone to serve their interests with an eloquent speech delivered by one Major Cassius Starbuckle (John Carradine). From his name, accent, and clothing, Starbuckle clearly was a major in the Confederate army, which tells us much of what we need to know about the (unseen) ranchers' motives.

When his friends nominate Stoddard, Starbuckle leaps to his feet and opposes the nomination on the grounds that Stoddard's only qualification "is that he killed man." Stoddard is shamed by this and retreats to a side office. Doniphon finds him there, and this is the moment where he tells Stoddard that he, Doniphon, killed Liberty from the alley. Stoddard recovers his courage. He does not, as Starbuckle declared, have "the mark of Cain" on him after all. He resolves to go back into the convention, and the larger flashback finally ends with the sight of Stoddard returning to become the people's representative as Jimmy Stewart's voiceover tells us that he went on not only to win statehood for the territory but also to become its first governor and then a senator. He has, in other words, spent his whole life as a representative.

With Liberty Valance already dead, what is the point of this scene? Are Stoddard and Starbuckle the same? Both are playing parts that they know, in some sense, to be a sham. Starbuckle pretends to speak from the heart when in fact his words are prepackaged and the audience is in no doubt that he has been well paid by the ranchers. Stoddard takes on the role of "the man who shot Liberty Valance," and he cannot give it up without giving up the authority (or the rewards) it has conferred on him. Some have concluded from this that the film means to condemn all politicians and all fakery in favor of Doniphon's "chivalry" or "honesty," and also simply to decry the decline of the Old West and its code of honor. But this interpretation entirely misses the costs involved for Ransom and Hallie.

René Girard famously describes a sacrifice as an act with two faces, "appearing at times as a sacred obligation to be neglected at grave peril, at other times as a sort of criminal activity."[38] It is clear enough that Doniphon has performed such an act, one of fraternal solidarity or murder, depending on your perspective. Here, Stoddard's political career takes on a parallel aspect—it is both a fraud based on a lie as well as a duty to others that must, for the sake of society, be performed.[39]

Ransom wins political office and power but has to live with the permanent consciousness of being an actor, as heavy a burden in its own way as Doniphon's decline into obscurity. Every time he hears his moniker (which is often), he is reminded of his status as an impostor. This is the bitterness inevitably tied to the sweetness of his erotic connection. He has to perform, to not be his natural self—*and not just a single time, as Doniphon did, but for an entire lifetime*. He is able to do this, though, and he does it for Hallie's sake. But that does not mean he enjoys it. At the beginning, he is an enthusiast for the law and education—glibly telling Hallie, for example, that he can teach her to read "in no time" and that it will transform her life—and earnestly promising the townspeople "progress." By the end, however, the law and the freedom he has won for himself and others afford him no joy. He has shed his optimism, we might say, and become a democratic pessimist, having learned that freedom and happiness are at odds with one another.[40] Tellingly, a ransom is the price one held hostage by crime pays to go free, and we are reluctant to pay (among other reasons) because to do so seems to validate the crime. The price of freedom here is a sacrifice of dignity and happiness that Ransom pays, in his own way, as much as Tom does. The erotic bond that holds them together as a community and ensures their freedom exacts a tribute.

Stoddard and Starbuckle are contrasts not on the point of being actors but on the point of having a conscience. Stoddard is one of Rousseau's honest actors. His knowledge of what he has and *hasn't* done keeps him tethered to reality so that he doesn't become Starbuckle, who has lost all sense of himself.[41] He is indebted to Doniphon for his life and his station, and the debt can never be discharged. Dorothy Johnson's story emphasizes how Doniphon *is* Stoddard's conscience (reminding him, from time to time, where his duty lies), but the last scene in the movie shows as well how the conscience outlives Doniphon and has become part of Stoddard's (second, civil) nature. Stoddard is tied to those he speaks for not by his honesty or good will (or money or power) but by an erotic debt of identity that ensures, as nothing else could, that he speaks as the genuine representative of his community.

Stoddard, like Doniphon, has to sacrifice his natural identity in order for others to live in peace and security in a state. That is the price Ransom, the first citizen, pays. He pays this price not for money, nor because he is selfless, but because of his commitment to Hallie. It was his erotic commitment that kept him in the town when any cost-benefit analysis would have told him to leave. Without an erotic engagement, the coordination of force and law cannot begin. And without a narrative, as I argue later, that coordination cannot continue. But the civic freedom it brings must be its own reward; happiness is not part of the bargain.

THE THIRD SHOOTER

Hannah Arendt famously quoted Isak Dinesen at the beginning of the "Action" chapter of *The Human Condition*: "All sorrows can be borne if you can put them into a story."[42] The story of the end of Liberty is an erotic one, but it is the narrative that makes the individual relationships into a lasting constellation of political consequence. Both fact and legend, the narrative of *The Man Who Shot Liberty Valance* creates us as the inheritors of a violent past that we can choose to acknowledge or, like the newspaper editor, choose to ignore. We cannot undo the violence that has created and sustained the democracy we enjoy, and neither can we legalize it—any more than the original participants could—but perhaps we can *bear* to live with its memory if we come to believe that its origin was not selfish but shared and burdensome to those who perpetrated it, that it was not just an arbitrary decision to exclude but also a creative and collective act of union.

The *story* of the man who shot Liberty is not something that the facts themselves could somehow conjure into existence. For this, we need a third "shooter"—in this case, the filmmaker, who is able to make the bare actions of individuals into a coherent narrative that supports the town's existence as a sovereign entity of law. This narration in some sense replicates or perpetuates the binding-by-separating function of Hallie's love. It is her relationship with both men that ensures, for everyone else in the town, that they have not acted selfishly, for their own motives (e.g., to become powerful or famous, etc.), and that the shooting has the proper *meaning*—the establishment of law and not just, as it could mean, the continuation of rule by the gun. It is the *story* of the death of Liberty, not the bullet that kills him, that ensures the state of law continues past its founding moments. If we are sustained, in any way, by this narrative, it is the third shooter who has provided us with something of political value, not the (fictional) characters who fired (fictional) weapons. Eros makes the narrative, and the narrative makes the state. And narrative is neither reason nor power, but something that binds them together into an action with a meaning that can be perpetuated to an audience.

I do not mean to suggest here that the film's narrative is trying to (or somehow could) justify all the violence in the American past (its attention to continuing inequality, I believe, is evidence enough of that). The story actually represents an ideal case with a perfectly vicious enemy and asks whether *any* kind of extra-legal exclusion in state-making can *ever* be acknowledged by a law-bound polity. Dinesen may have been wrong to suggest that *all* sorrows can be borne in such a fashion, but Ford's film shows how *some* sorrows *might* be. Arendt was not wrong to argue that deeds become part of a polity's identity when they are remembered and retold—that power and law cannot perpetuate their authority without a narrative.[43] But even in ideal cases, such incorporation comes with a price to all involved.

PARADOX AND PESSIMISM

The democratic paradox is actually made more paradoxical when we allow our ordinary expectations about representation and sovereignty to become distorted by an excess of optimism. Mouffe argues that coming to terms with the paradox means "[c]oming to terms with the constitutive nature of power [and] relinquishing the ideal of a democratic society as the realization of a perfect harmony or transparency."[44] *Liberty Valance* gives us a concrete example of what that process might look like. The optimist presumes that there must be some way for our freedom to not be linked to suffering—whether of others or of ourselves. If instead we recognize, as the pessimists recognize, that freedom and happiness are in tension, then the situation is less paradoxical and more political. We can only choose freedom, as founders might have, knowing it will burden others and ourselves. If we cannot relieve freedom of its continuing burden of exclusion, we can at least acknowledge that we have done so and make what amends are possible.

The ending of the film is notably ambivalent. Ransom and Hallie board a train back to Washington. The conductor explains how the railway is holding an express train in St. Louis so that the Senator can return to Washington that much faster. Ransom strikes a match and is about to light his pipe as he thanks the conductor. When the conductor replies "Nothing's too good for the man who shot Liberty Valance," Ransom pauses and then blows out the match and puts down the unlit pipe—he and Hallie stare blankly ahead. The freedom they have won is not crowned by happiness—indeed, they are constantly reminded of what they have lost and have not even the oblivion afforded to Doniphon for relief. Ransom must always play the part of the shooter. Hallie is haunted by the man she could not keep. The sadness on their faces is not only for the unremembered Doniphon; it is also for themselves.

If the only loss, in establishing a representative democracy, were the death of obnoxious villains like Valance, the choice would be a relatively easy one. But as we have seen, Valance is not the only one who pays. In this film, more plausibly, civic freedom comes with a visible and continuing cost—one paid not only by those excluded but by all who participate in the act of exclusion as well. Perhaps this is why, as several critics have noted, post-statehood Shinbone seems to be a quiet, lifeless town compared to the boisterous, diverse encampment of its earlier days.[45]

Optimistic democrats like Habermas, and even Connolly and Honig to a degree, want the future to make up for the past. The sense of *Liberty Valance* is that it never will. But at the same time, it shows that setting the fact alongside the legend does not destroy the democratic state or its legitimacy, as someone like Schmitt or Agamben thinks it must. The film gives the lie to a promise of "progress for the future" that optimists wrongly believe to be a necessary supplement to modern democracy, yet without falling back into the Schmittian position that exclusion is the essence of the state. It takes up the challenge of Mouffe and Honig to endure the paradox without paying off the debt it creates with a currency from the future. The state is depicted as the bittersweet, constitutive merging of law and power enacted by humans bound together by erotic forces. Whether it was worth it is a question always to be answered in the present by an audience that receives this state as a narrative inheritance and has to decide whether to reprint it.

It is no wonder Ford's film, even with its all-star cast, was unpopular.[46] Asking an audience not simply to acknowledge foundational violence but to accept responsibility for sustaining its effects may be mature and even patriotic. Only individuals of a peculiar temperament, however, would find it entertaining. As Rousseau pointed out long ago, to expect a theatrical audience to enjoy hearing the truth about themselves is to court commercial failure. At best, one might hope, with Girard, for a condition in which the *demos* of a modern state "is both attracted and repelled by its own origins."[47] If the film is a favorite of political theorists, this is because it asks and answers fundamental questions about the nature of sovereign democracy. While the film does not dissolve the paradox, it suggests a pessimistic way of working through it without avoiding its most painful aspects.

Asking who really shot Liberty Valance is like asking whether George Washington or Thomas Jefferson is the true author of the American Republic. Such a question can only be answered: not one man or one act, but only humans together can make a state. They can only make a state of law by excluding other humans and by sacrificing part of themselves in that exclusion. It is eros that unites them and a story that sustains their union—not through a miraculous act of ratiocination or decision, but simply through a capacity to dissolve boundaries (between individuals, between law and power, between this moment and the next one) that otherwise seem static and impermeable. The Man Who Shot Liberty Valance is like one of those strange creatures from Plato's *Symposium* who has found its other half. And of course, like all erotic seekers, having found what it has searched for it is inevitably disappointed by wholeness. States are sustained by our endurance of that disappointment.

In the first moments of the film, when Ransom and Hallie return to Shinbone, the camera takes their perspective, and we see Doniphon as they do: through a doorway but in a rough-hewn pine box, with the doorframe marking the boundary between life and death. Even after Doniphon's death, Ransom and Hallie feel obliged by his memory. Ransom's service as representative is not even ended by the demise of his constituent. Obviously, this has nothing to do with an electoral mandate, but it has everything to do with how we might conceive of a representative condition whose legitimacy exceeds what epistemic models of representation can offer. Although Doniphon is past speaking, Ransom's continued service gives voice to the meaning of his actions and his being. If preservation in the face of death is to be anything other than vain memorialization, perhaps it can best arise in this kind of representation, one bound by a community-forging debt and carried as a burden by its inheritors. I will return to this question in the conclusion (Chapter 6).

[4]

REPRESENTING EVIL

Von Trier's Werewolves

Evil presents a peculiar problem for any theory of representation, aesthetic or political. Granted that evil exists in the world and in any population, is a representation better for including it or for avoiding it? Our ordinary commitment to representative fidelity looks peculiar in the case of evil. Do we want representative art, or politics, to reflect the world by including evil, or is one of the virtues of representation that the effects of evil can be reduced or avoided by preventing their reproduction? The difficulty of these questions is multiplied by long-standing debates about the nature of evil itself.[1]

In Augustine's famous formula, evil is the privation, or absence, of good. This suggests that evil might pose a particular problem for a filmmaker who is devoted to grappling with it. Absence is something we cannot actually see; it must be inferred from the presence of something else. The principle implies that evil can defy direct representation, whether in discourse or on film. If Augustine is right, then we might expect evil to appear only indirectly, or by extraordinary means, in conventional films or politics.

If, on the other hand, we reject Augustine and take evil to be routinely manifest—not absent or hidden at all—then we might think that no exceptional techniques are needed to make it visible or to secure its presence on film. Indeed, in this case, the best way to capture evil might be through the simplest practices, where the filmmaker's contrivance is letting the images, unmanipulated and unstaged, speak for themselves.

Cinema Pessimism. Joshua Foa Dienstag, Oxford University Press (2020).

DOI: 10.1093/oso/9780190067717.001.0001

Somewhere between these two positions lies the work of Lars von Trier. Over and over, his films depict a world in which evil is omnipresent and yet difficult, but not impossible, to see directly. This difficulty is depicted by various techniques and often through the varied reactions of his characters to their circumstances. Despite the fact that they all live in the same world and experience the same (often horrible) events, some von Trier characters remain blind to the evil that surrounds them, while others, usually his heroines (or anti-heroines), see more clearly what is not apparent to others (or to the audience).

In his films, von Trier repeatedly takes the side of those who see evil, who refuse what we can call cinema optimism, which sees a better world in place of the one that actually exists. In fact, he is generally suspicious of film itself since that medium is so often complicit in this optimism, which replaces an honest look at the evil world as it truly exists with an imaginary world of pleasant fantasy (e.g., the Hollywood romantic comedy). And yet, as von Trier's filmmaking has evolved in recent years, he has proved more and more willing to make use of advanced illusive filmmaking techniques (e.g., special effects and computer-generated images) that he once scorned. Among other things, this chapter explores this evolution to see if it holds any lessons for the way we engage in politics.

In every perspective on the representability of evil, a politics is implied. The view that evil is a blatant presence in the world calls for its direct confrontation. Augustine's view of evil as absence must take another route and often thinks of evil as an error to be avoided or as an emptiness to be filled with good works. But von Trier's conception of evil as something that is hard, but not impossible, to see has particular implications for our ideas of representation, and it assigns special responsibility to representation in political life.

It also challenges our understanding of what a good representation is, and even what representation in politics might be for. Theories of political representation do not often grapple with the idea that the evil which lurks in any people is worthy of representation, or in need of it. If anything, representation is often assumed to be a system of filtration where the ignorance or prejudice of the multitude can be restrained by the educated judgment of its representatives. Even when radical democrats complain that a people's diversity is not fully represented, they do not usually have the moral diversity of that people in mind. But no theory of democratic representation can be complete unless it considers the evil that exists in any population and how that evil stands in relation to its representatives and representations. Against the optimism of some Hollywood cinema, von Trier develops an important element of cinema pessimism by insisting on the representation of an evil that escapes our ordinary vision.[2]

In this chapter, I focus largely on *Europa* (1991)[3] and *Melancholia* (2011). Both films grapple with the question of evil and the difficulty of seeing or representing it. Each features two main characters: one who remains blind to an evil that is pervasive and another who sees it, or who sees it part of time. Von Trier links the capacity to see evil with the quality of being part animal. Animals, for von Trier, are far from innocent creatures but rather tend to know something about the malevolence of the world that humans do not. Perhaps because wolves in particular have vision that is adapted to the nighttime, von Trier turns to them to explore what they can see that is invisible to the rest of us. By way of these evil-seeing characters, he offers what I will call a *werewolf perspective.*

Beyond his films, von Trier is well-known for the strong statements about filmmaking contained in the founding documents of the Dogma 95 movement. As I discuss later, those writings display a hostility toward illusion and a devotion to a particular approach to fiction filmmaking. But as his own work has evolved, I maintain, he has more clearly adopted a pessimistic perspective, which was initially the special privilege of his werewolf characters. To confront evil through the medium of film, von Trier's late work adopts techniques and perspectives that his younger self might have decried. His reasons for doing so are as much moral and ontological as they are aesthetic.

How, von Trier asks, can one be a citizen or representative in a world that is permanently polluted by evil? Seeing evil takes a special kind of vision, adapted to evil's status as something omnipresent but fugitive. And if evil is fugitive, then its representation can never be realistic. This is not just an aesthetic proposition but also a political one, an important element of cinema pessimism.

THE EVILS OF REPRESENTATION

Von Trier's initial hostility to filmic artifice and illusion is clearly displayed in the two original documents of the Dogma 95 group that he co-founded with fellow Danish director Thomas Vinterberg. "To Dogma 95," the two wrote in their Manifesto, "the movie is not illusion!"[4] The eleven edicts contained in their Vow of Chastity (the second document) are essentially a promise to make fiction films according to rules that seem designed to minimize artifice—no music, no distortions of light or sound, use only of handheld cameras, all shooting done on location, and all plots to take place in the historical present. The tenth rule says that "the director must not be credited." And the eleventh rule explains why: "I swear as a director to refrain from personal taste! I am no longer an artist. I swear to refrain from creating a 'work,' as I regard the instant as more important than the whole. My supreme goal is to force the truth out of my characters and settings. I swear to do so by all the means available and at the cost of any good taste and any aesthetic considerations."[5]

Although the Dogma 95 group made fictional films, its original statements reflect a commitment to a seemingly anti-artistic style, akin in some respects to Italian neorealism. According to von Trier and Vinterberg, distortion and illusion are something introduced by filmmakers seeking to be "artistic," or by Hollywood in its crass quest to commercialize entertainment.[6] The task of filmmakers, according to these documents, is to remove themselves as much as possible from the process in order to let the world (as a succession of instants) appear directly to the camera, whether beautiful or ugly, good or evil. The director, that is, should not be an artist but only a truth-seeker. While von Trier and Vinterberg were probably never themselves as naïve and simplistic as their manifesto (they have said that they intended it as an extreme statement designed to provoke), their suspicion of cinematic techniques and artistry was very real. Dogma 95 in no way opposed the making of fiction film, but it distinguished what I would call the fictions of the writer from the illusions of the director and/or cinematographer.[7]

Von Trier and Vinterberg celebrated the democratization of film through the availability of cheap cameras and digital recording. But they also worried about the newly and easily available techniques of cinematic artifice—what once was the province of special-effects departments in studios or expensive cameras and lenses can now be duplicated by anyone with a laptop. And if everyone is an artist, then no one is left to document the truth: "By using new technology anyone at any time can wash the last grains of truth away in the deadly embrace of sensation. The illusions are everything the movie can hide behind."[8] A true movie ("*the* movie," as they call it), in these documents, is a photoplay that eschews cinematic illusion and concentrates entirely on setting, character, and dialogue.

Within the constraints of fiction, then, Dogma 95 was committed to as unmediated a form of representation as a filmmaker could manage, with good or evil coming to light in whatever proportion they appeared before the camera. Von Trier and Vinterberg were distressed, to say the least, by the possibility that representation may beautify what exists in the world in the first place. But over time, to von Trier, the representation of only what is naturally visible began to seem morally inadequate.

As is well-known, von Trier made just one film that fully complies with Dogma 95's rules (*The Idiots* in 1998). Nevertheless, he has retained a kind of dedication to its larger challenge: The best cinema is anti-cinema, something that is either not an illusion at all, or is an illusion that deconstructs its illusory status and debunks itself as it goes along. But that dedication is tested in the films where he faces the problem of an evil that retreats, or hides, from view. One can point the camera at violence, poverty, cruelty, and suffering—and von Trier often does this—but to point it at evil is more of a challenge.

In *Europa,* he introduces a character who has a vision of evil that we, the audience, do not; in *Melancholia,* von Trier tries to share that perspective with his audience, at the cost, perhaps, of becoming the kind of "artist" he denounced in 1995. He also asks us, in effect, to reconsider what it means for representation to be adequate to a world permeated by evil.

EUROPA: POLITICAL EVIL

Europa was made before the Dogma 95 manifesto was written and does not conform to its principles. But *Europa* makes heavy use of the second path to anti-cinema: even as it tells a fictional story, it relentlessly calls attention to itself as a film through a variety of techniques that disrupt the viewer's suspension of disbelief—most notably through a jarring mix of black-and-white and color film stock that make the characters appear as if they are dropping in and out of different movies.[9] There is also a voice-over narration that speaks directly to the audience and depicts the film as a kind of hypnotic dream. The story begins with a view of train tracks—shot from a moving train so that they look like a filmstrip—while the narrator says things like "I will now count to ten . . . On the mental count of ten you will be in Europa. Be there at ten. I say: ten." The audience is thus repeatedly reminded that what it is seeing is an illusion or dream of some kind.[10]

Set in the fall of 1945, *Europa* tells the tragicomic story of Leopold Kessler, an American of German descent who has come to Germany to work (as a civilian) for a railway company called Zentropa.[11] Kessler has no sympathy for Nazism, but as a pacifist, he refused to participate in the war. When asked his reasons for coming to Germany, he says, in apparent seriousness, "It's about time someone showed this country a little kindness."

Kessler meets Katherine Hartmann, the daughter of the family that owns the Zentropa train company.[12] The company is under pressure both from the occupation authorities that want its resources to rebuild Germany and from the Werewolves, Hitler loyalists who want to attack the occupation.[13] Kessler falls in love with Katherine and marries her shortly after these conflicting forces drive her father to commit suicide. In the end, Katherine is herself revealed to be a Werewolf, and she and Kessler are killed when a Werewolf bomb that she planted goes off and plunges their railway car into a river.

The real subject of *Europa* is the evil of Nazism and our response to it. But the Nazis themselves remain off-camera. We see no German soldiers; instead, the uniforms of the railway employees look menacingly fascist. We see no atrocities, but Kessler is subjected to a bizarre medical exam before being allowed to join the railway company, as if he were in a camp. The trains themselves, of course, are a constant reminder of genocide since, as everybody knows (and as von Trier shows us in one dream-like sequence), they were used to transport millions to their deaths.

Kessler himself, however, is strangely or willfully blind to these associations.[14] When ominous things happen, he says they can be "easily explained." When his sinister uncle says, "There is nothing to see," Kessler doesn't question it. And when the railway regulations require absurd acts, he does not object—not until the last moments of the film.

How, then, should we view Kessler, a pacifist in principle but obstinately ignorant about the evils around him? Two incidents are suggestive. One is a scene in which Kessler and a priest are discussing the issue of responsibility and forgiveness. The priest says, "God is on everybody's side. But when you fight for a cause with all your heart, God finds it easier to forgive." When Kessler asks if there is anyone God can't forgive, the priest says, "The unbelievers. The lukewarm ones who don't take sides. They are condemned to eternal wandering. He has no mercy on them, Herr Kessler. 'So because thou art lukewarm, I will spit thee out of my mouth.'"[15]

The priest does not direct this judgment at Kessler, but Katherine does in the second incident, her final conversation with him. After her Werewolf identity has been revealed, she tells him, "The way I see it is that you are the only criminal." When he protests—"I haven't done anything! I'm not working for either side!"—she responds, "Exactly." In Katherine's judgment, to take no side is itself a sin. To be blind to evil is at least as bad, if not worse (and this is the part that is hard to swallow) than evil itself. Katherine does not really defend the justice of the Nazi cause—she only defends choosing a side, and indeed, when Kessler points out that bombing the train will kill many Germans, she says, "What people? Everybody on this train has been through the war just like me. You can't compare yourself to us. Everybody here has killed or betrayed, directly or indirectly, hundreds of times, just to survive."

Kessler's vision, however, is beyond repair. He wears glasses throughout the film (which von Trier often calls attention to) and still does not see evil as he should. As a character, Kessler himself is a kind of zero, a man with no perspective. His love for Katherine is not really explained, and it would be hard to explain as an independent emotion—it seems more like a reflection of Katherine's love for him. She is the one who first proposes sex and then marriage. Thus, Kessler is not only a pacifist, but a passivist. When he complains at the end of the film that "I've got this rotten feeling that everyone's been screwing me ever since I got here," we feel little sympathy for him since he seems to have so little personality himself.

Kessler has been like a documentary camera: through him, we see everyone reveal themselves, and almost all reveal themselves to be agents of a larger, unseen evil—the ruthless occupiers and the ex-Nazis. And yet Kessler himself is blind to what is all around him. He is in Germany in late 1945 but does not seem to notice that he is surrounded by murderers. His "kindness" and pacifism make him oblivious to what Katherine perceives very clearly—namely, that she is surrounded by an evil no one wants to talk about. Indeed, she feels that it is impossible not to participate in it; only the blind can remain lukewarm.

Katherine's status as a werewolf, however, is much more than being a Nazi sympathizer. By way of excusing her marriage to Kessler, which she insists was not part of her plot, she describes herself as a genuinely divided being: "Please believe me when I tell you I really cared for you. . . . You know, they say a werewolf is only a werewolf at night. In the daytime, it's a human being. I know I can't make you understand what it is that makes a man turn into an animal because you don't accept that it ever happens. During nights I wrote the [threatening] letters to father. During days, I regretted it."

For Katherine, being a werewolf (or Werewolf) is like having a kind of second, animal sight or perspective that supplements, without entirely replacing, her first. "Animal" here seems to signal a malevolence that humans want to deny is part of their nature but that is visible in Nazism and other human horrors. The werewolf perspective enables Katherine, especially at night, to see the evil in the world and to recognize her own part in it. She acts based on her knowledge of that evil, of the fact that it is widespread and, perhaps, even universal. She doesn't claim innocence for herself—just a shared guilt with her victims. To pretend otherwise is to her a kind of dishonesty. Kessler, to the end, cannot understand her perspective.

If there is a flaw in *Europa*, it is that the film does not make this dual werewolf perspective of Katherine's directly available to the audience. We only hear her description of it. Katherine is both a representative and a representation of the evil of Naziism. But the audience can neither see that evil by looking at Katherine directly, nor can we see the world as she sees it. The film's disruptive cinematography only reminds the audience of the potentially deceptive nature of what they are watching; it does not give us access to Katherine's point of view. Insofar as its unconventional elements offer a substitute for established forms of representation, it is hard to imagine how they could be translated into a political practice. But in *Melancholia,* as we shall see, a different kind of alternative is presented.

SEEING EVIL

Kessler and Katherine are a pair that von Trier repeats over and over: a man who cannot see evil or rationalizes away what he sees, and a woman who sees evil clearly and is identified with it. Kessler believes that his refusal to take sides is a kind of objectivity or justice. But *Europa* depicts him instead as naïve, willfully blind—indeed, even as criminal. He/She in *Antichrist* and Seligman/Joe in *Nymphomania* also fit this pattern.[16] Yet in *Melancholia,* as we shall see, things are more complicated.

In his essay "On a Certain Blindness in Human Beings," William James laments our inability to see the world from the perspective of others and the value in things that others find.[17] James is largely referring to the subjective "joy" we take in items or events that others cannot appreciate. George Kateb, who recurs to James's essay, refers also to our capacity for "moral blindness" as another result of this inability. "Almost no one," he writes, "grants equal reality to others," with disastrous consequences for moral reasoning and politics.[18] While this problem is in one sense ineradicable—we will never truly see the world from the perspective of someone else—in another sense, Kateb argues, it may at least be combatted by a certain kind of imaginative education: "When one is morally blind, one refuses to allow the present to be present; one keeps it out of sight . . . With the exercise of imagination, another person can at least be understood as real."[19] But what sort of imagination is required?

In *Europa,* the camera's perspective reproduces Kessler's blind objectivity. We see strange things happen that we cannot (or *will* not) understand. The world is opaque, and evil lurks everywhere but is invisible to us. What, then, would it take for us to see "the present as present," to see the world from Katherine's werewolf perspective? James and Kateb suggest a *purposefully subjective* form of representation, one that reproduces a personal point of view, as the potential cure for moral blindness. We must see the world as *someone* sees it, rather than as no one sees it, in order to see morally. This suggests that the Dogma approach—in seeking a kind of anti-subjectivity—is nonetheless missing something real and important.

Von Trier took some time to realize this. If he did not strictly adhere to the rules outlined in Dogma 95's Vow of Chastity after *The Idiots*, his films in the 1990s and early 2000s still reflected its spirit. *Breaking the Waves* (1996) and *Dancer in the Dark* (2003) abandoned *Europa*'s stylized tricks with film stock, color, sets, and lighting and were instead shot on location with handheld cameras and little cinematic embellishment. *Dogville* (2003) and *Manderlay* (2005) were shot on soundstages with minimal props, sets, background music, or other elements of cinematic illusion. The emphasis in these films is almost entirely on the actors, dialogue, and action—a style that won von Trier many awards and a distinctive reputation.

Beginning with *Antichrist* (2009), however, von Trier's films begin, once again, to use complex, expensive, technology-intensive cinematic techniques, though now rather different from those used in *Europa*. While *Europa*'s distortions seem designed to keep the film's status as a film in the forefront of the viewer's mind, the later films use special effects and illusions less disruptively, in the service of a story. Like *Europa*, these later films are preoccupied with the ubiquity of evil and with the women and men who see it or who fail to (respectively). In the later films, however, von Trier allows viewers to see the world the way a werewolf would see it. And the werewolf perspective is not just described. It is shown: a vision where evil routinely appears.

In place of the earlier film's self-announcing techniques, which call attention to the medium, the later films use subtler methods to present nature in its most "unnatural" and grotesque forms—often (though not always) at night. Thus, *Antichrist* shows misshapen animals, *Nymphomania* reveries, and *Melancholia* fantastic cosmological events. But we come to this vision neither by avoiding optical illusions and cinematic flourishes nor by prohibiting directorial artistry. Von Trier seems to have conceded that to see the world "objectively" is to see it as his blind male characters do. To film it morally, and to bring evil into view, he now resorts to cinematic artifice and special effects; indeed, at times, he revels in them. In sum, the representation on display in these films actually *increases* the visibility of evil and makes it *more* visible than it is in the everyday world (or in the view of the documentary camera).

MELANCHOLIA: RADICAL EVIL

"The Earth is evil," says Justine toward the end of what is undoubtedly von Trier's most beautiful and artificial film, *Melancholia*. Why, we might ask, if the Earth is so evil, does von Trier depict it so gorgeously, using all the latest film techniques to do so? In *Europa*, the physical environment is for the most part creepy, menacing, and full of shadows. *Melancholia*, by contrast, is full of luscious colors, artful tableaux, exquisite costumes, and in general, beautiful filmmaking. It is as if von Trier has taken up the theme of *Europa* from a completely opposite cinematic perspective—and as if the evil of Nazism were no longer a large enough topic, so *Melancholia*'s subject is the evil of our species and planet.

In formal, cinematic terms, the opening minutes of *Melancholia* could almost be taken as a point-by-point repudiation of every rule in the Vow of Chastity. As the overture from Wagner's *Tristan und Isolde* plays loudly, we see a series of highly stylized, digitally altered images. Some move in a super-slow motion, and others are still but gorgeously composed. Still others enact physically impossible, dream-like moments that will figure later in the story. It is all capped off with computer-generated images that take an unearthly perspective and reveal the ending of the preposterous, operatic plot of the movie: Earth is destroyed when it collides with another, much larger planet named Melancholia.[20] Everyone dies, and all life on the planet is exterminated. And according to Justine, justly so.

The film tells the story of the Earth's last days from the perspective of two sisters, Claire and Justine. In the first half of the film, we see the evening of Justine's wedding. She is trying to fit into a world for which she is profoundly unsuited. Against her better judgment, she is marrying a cheerful man and is letting her sister and her sister's husband throw them a luxurious wedding. But the evening goes from bad to worse as Justine becomes more and more disengaged from the event, her family, and even her spouse. By the end of the wedding reception, she has lost her job, her marriage, and has alienated her family. As the rogue planet Melancholia appears and begins heading toward Earth, she seems to sink into a catatonic depression.

The second half of the film begins with Claire unsuccessfully attempting to lift Justine's spirits. Then, as Melancholia comes closer to Earth, Justine begins to revive. Claire's husband, John, as optimistic as Justine is pessimistic, is convinced that the two planets will fly harmlessly past one another; Claire is more worried. When it becomes clear that a collision will occur, John kills himself, and Claire becomes distraught. Justine, however, is calm and collected and helps Claire and her son prepare for the inevitable.

Melancholia, like *Europa* and other Von Trier films, does feature a morally blind man—Claire's husband. John is rich and has paid for the lavish wedding, somewhat unwillingly. His first words to Justine about it are "You better be goddamn happy," to which Justine replies, "Yes, I should be. I really should be." John views the world clinically, scientifically, but also (and as a result) optimistically—he likes to look at Melancholia through an expensive telescope that he has bought and that he doesn't let others touch. When Claire asks him why he is so sure that there is no danger, he says, "You have to trust the scientists." He prepares for the planetary flyby methodically, stocking up on food and cooking gas. He looks forward to it as a thrilling but manageable adventure that he wants to share with his wife and son. But when he realizes that the scientists have miscalculated, he abruptly runs off and commits suicide, abandoning his family. Without a positive narrative to sustain him, he can find nothing to live for.

The main contrast that the film draws is not between John and Justine, however, but between Justine and Claire. Claire neither shares her husband's technophilia nor his optimism, but she is nevertheless Justine's opposite. Von Trier has assigned the "scientific" elements of the modern worldview onto the character of John in order to focus on the remaining characteristics that distinguish the two sisters.

After the elaborate overture, the film is divided into two chapters that are simply titled "Justine" and "Claire." Several writers have pointed out that the first chapter, which covers the day of Justine's wedding, does conform to many of the Dogma 95 precepts, including a great deal of handheld cinematography.[21] The second chapter, by contrast, contains many formal compositions and special-effects sequences that illustrate the strange, looming planet and the impact of its approach on Earth. An obvious explanation suggests itself: von Trier is illustrating the two ways of looking at the world—the Dogma style of the first half is contrasted with the stylized cinematic perspective in the second. Recall that Katherine Hartman claimed that she had two ways of looking at the world that alternated between day and night. Here too we see the lunar perspective and the solar. But what is the significance of this new (for von Trier) style of cinematography? To answer this question, it is necessary to understand something more about what it is Justine sees that the rest of us ordinarily do not.

"Melancholia" is an old word, originating in Greek; it initially referred to an excess of the black bile that was thought to emanate from the spleen. But the four humors—of which black bile is one—were also associated with the four elements (earth/air/fire/water), and black bile was linked to earth. Thus, a melancholic could be said to be someone *too full of the earth*. Over the centuries, of course, the word has acquired a more psychological meaning, and today, that meaning is the dominant one. But Justine's "illness" (as well as her vision) reflects the older understanding, while her sister insists on seeing her symptoms through the modern one. The two sisters thus understand melancholy (and Melancholia) according to two very different frames of meaning.

Claire treats her sister's condition psychologically. She describes Justine as "depressed" and tries to cheer her up by providing joyful experiences: she makes her sister's favorite meal, draws her bath, and takes her riding on her favorite horse. These efforts don't work (Justine says the meatloaf "tastes like ashes," won't get into the bath, and then beats her horse cruelly), but the point is that Claire treats the "melancholy" at a mental level, and a shallow one at that—she can only understand her sister's dark thoughts as a psychological disturbance that might be cured by pleasant episodes.

Some writers on the film have thus taken Claire's perspective when they describe the planet Melancholia as a metaphor for Justine's depression, and the film itself as an exploration of von Trier's own depression (which he has discussed in various interviews).[22] But such critics fail to take seriously—almost as if they cannot bring themselves to believe it—the possibility that what Justine says about the Earth is true. She says, "The Earth is evil; we don't need to grieve for it." And through her the film does the unthinkable: it really does contemplate the end of the world as a good thing (something else that von Trier has explicitly described).[23]

This contemplation of evil is performed by a character with a twofold, werewolf perspective: Justine is a direct descendant of Katherine from *Europa*. We can see this clearly in a striking episode about three-quarters of the way through the film. As the planet Melancholia approaches, Justine has become more revived. In a scene full of special effects, von Trier creates a tableau where the new planet, because of its distance from Earth, appears to be the same size as the moon. The two "moons" thus appear in the same night sky, with Melancholia giving off a blue light that contrasts with the ordinary moon's yellow light.

Animated by the light of these moons, Justine, *like a werewolf*, sneaks away and (as her sister looks on surreptitiously) disrobes to absorb, especially, the unnatural moonlight of Melancholia. (We see her suffused in a purely blue light.) The expression on her face indicates that this moonlight-bathing is an erotic experience—a consummation of her relationship with the deadly planet. Claire watches but clearly doesn't understand. Why does her sister prefer a blue moon to her favorite meatloaf?

The answer, I argue, is that Justine's melancholy is neither chemical (as John might believe) nor psychological. It is ontological and moral. Justine is full of earth, and the Earth, as she says, is evil. The planet Melancholia—blue like the Earth, but much larger—is like her missing other half. (I am thinking here of the missing half from the Aristophanic description of eros in Plato's *Symposium*.) It will reunite with her and in doing so destroy her, and this Justine finds satisfying because it fulfills her desire to see evil acknowledged and punished, *including the evil in herself*. Her melancholy is thus less a psychological state than a sign of her werewolf perspective.[24]

Justine is not a Nazi, but like Katherine, Justine sees the world (and herself) full of unalterable evil. The impending collision therefore seems welcome, a fair judgment of the planet and a desirable release from its grip. Like Katherine, who has no regrets about everyone on the train (of Germany) dying, Justine has no qualms about her traveling companions on this planet. And like Katherine, hers is a kind of second sight. When Claire asks Justine how she knows (before anyone else does) that the planets will collide, she simply says that she "knows things" and, to prove it, then correctly names the number of beans in a jar at her wedding ("678"), something she could not possibly have known through ordinary means. She also knows there is no other life in the universe, she says, so that when our planet perishes, that will be the end of all life anywhere.

Justine's melancholia thus turns out to be a kind of lycanthropy, and its primary symptom, as with Katherine, is that she sees the evil in the world through a kind of second sight that she shares with animals. (The being that Justine is closest to in the film is her horse Abraham.) While this normally puts her at odds with the everyday world, in the special circumstances of an impending planetary collision she is, for the first time, in the driver's seat, well-equipped to cope with what others find terrifying. The difference from *Europa* is that this time the audience sees through both sets of eyes: first the ordinary human view, and then the werewolf perspective.

Should we be surprised that that the second viewpoint is the more beautiful one? Justine is a werewolf, and this is the world where she is at home. Is it surprising that it is attractive to her? Acknowledging its beauty in no way mitigates her moral condemnation, nor von Trier's. Indeed, it might even be said to correspond with von Trier's original condemnation of film artistry as immoral deception. If he seems to have become the artist he once condemned, it is important that his films' moral compasses still point in the same direction. *The wrongness of the beautiful world is undiminished*. In fact, its aesthetic attractiveness could even be the most dangerous part of evil. But von Trier has conceded that in order to depict evil, he must adopt the viewpoint *of someone who sees it* and *present it to his audience* by way of that perspective, even abandoning his signature, unadorned cinematography to do so. Like James and Kateb, *Melancholia* advocates for a morality derived not from objectivity, but from the subjective experience of individuals.

PESSIMISTIC REALISM

Many commentators have remarked on the fact that, as Melancholia approaches, Justine becomes more composed and Claire goes to pieces. When forced to live in a world of work and weddings—a progressive world of goals and accomplishments—Justine is hopelessly out of sync. But when impending death makes all human activities meaningless, Justine is finally in her element, and it is Claire who doesn't know how to function. We see here the incapacity of optimism to cope with a world that is fundamentally meaningless, and I don't think it is wrong to call Justine's perspective pessimistic and, more specifically, Schopenhauerian.[25]

We would already have the contrast of optimism and pessimism, however, between the two characters of Justine and John. So what, specifically, does the character of Claire, whose name means "light" and "clear" and titles the second half of the movie, have to add?

The irony of her name is that her vision is neither clear nor well-lit. Claire, *knowing what is about to happen, still acts as if her illusions ought to govern her behavior.* She wants the end of the world to be "nice," she says to Justine, pleading with her sister to face the end together with her, with wine and music. (Justine responds brutally that her sister's plan is "a piece of shit.") John's suicide was cowardly, but one could also say that it was his logical response to the facts, given his worldview. Claire—like Leopold Kessler—looks catastrophe in the face and can't quite admit it. There is *nothing* to be happy about when the world ends, and wine and music won't change that.

The optimism personified by John is not the only reason people fail to see what is right in front of them; Claire's blindness is different. Perhaps it is more like that cinema optimism that wants to project more goodness into every person and situation than is actually present, but it is no less blind.

Von Trier's decision to name a blind woman "Claire" also indicates something about his changing attitude toward "natural" representation. The original Dogma 95 rules demanded visual clarity: no distorting lenses or filters, no artificial lighting. But evil does not appear so easily, and our natural vision is too limited to see it. *That* blindness cannot be cured (as we might want to believe) by human caring, love, or empathy. Claire has these traits (which John lacks) in abundance, but they do not save her. Claire sees the world's beauty, clearly, as it were, and delights in its tangible pleasures, as her arrangement of the sumptuous wedding, with its visual, aural, and tactile elements makes plain. But Justine sees what Claire, and the Dogma camera, cannot—the emptiness that lies behind all that. Like Katherine, she has both a first and second sight, and the second tells her that what her first sight takes in is just an empty shell. Like Hamlet, the original melancholy Dane, Justine sees the play and the emptiness behind it at the same time.

The Dogma 95 rules require natural light because to film anything requires light ("*claire*"). If there is to be any kind of depiction of the world from Justine's perspective, as evil, it will *not* be something "clear" or realistic at all. It would have to appear, in effect, as something fantastic, or monstrous, or unreal—lit by an *unnatural light like the light of an unnatural moon. Melancholia* leaves behind the Dogma aesthetic of von Trier's earlier films for a different, pessimistic kind of realism, one that attempts to lead us to perceive a real emptiness that no natural light can illuminate. Thanks to a blue moon (i.e., "once in a blue moon"), we have the opportunity to see the world from the werewolf perspective.

Thus, the camera tricks and special effects that von Trier once eschewed because of their connection with cinema optimism are now repurposed for something very different: a pessimistic realism. Von Trier's goal of revealing the truth, even at the expense of our feelings, has not changed, but a recognition of the difficulty involved in meeting that goal has allowed, or forced, a change in means or technique. Even beauty and artistry, all the things that made representation so dangerous, can now be recruited into the project of representing evil through the perspective of the werewolf.

Some truths do not appear by natural light. Some representations omit because they only film what is manifestly present. *Melancholia* suggests that measuring the quality of a representation in terms of its faithfulness to what appears naturally is short-sighted (actually, blind-sighted). When evil is unspoken, hidden, or metaphysical, it will not readily appear before the camera. It needs to be coaxed into view and, perhaps, represented unnaturally. If this is an obligation of representation, it is not an obligation that can be established by our ordinary ideas of representative fidelity. But this also suggests that representation may have a hidden function that is brought to light when we consider its potential to expose what is hidden or hard to see.

REPRESENTING EVIL

To view an evil that is fugitive, something more than ordinary vision is required. The werewolf has two bodies, which means two sets of eyes and two sorts of visions: one for day, the other for night. By night, they see the hidden evil for what it is and do not obscure it with their own illusory projections or hopeful redemptions. Human cruelty, violence, and selfish sexuality are what exist, but we imagine them to be bounded or counterbalanced by some order, meaning, or goodness. To make a film without indulging such illusions has always been von Trier's intention. *Europa* and the rules of Dogma 95 were among his first efforts toward this end. His turn to new techniques, including some of those he once prohibited to himself, is a different effort in the same cause.

So the werewolf vision of von Trier's female characters is really a kind of parallax compliment: if we are to see things as they really are, we must adopt a second perspective, one that looks, from our present perspective, inhuman—but only because the place of humanity is taken up by *men* who lack vision or who see only in a conventional way. In these films at least, von Trier reverses the normal Hollywood pattern and depicts women as the more fully rounded creatures, while the men are incompletely human and (merely) male (or, perhaps, merely human, while the women are something more and better).[26] Perhaps we should simply say, more radically, that ordinary human vision will never be fully perceptive, and that the inhuman representation is the better one. Von Trier's initial suspicion of the director has been replaced with (or rather, generalized into) a hatred of the species.

There is a more general point here: Hollywood films do not display illusions simply because they employ special lenses, lighting, and computer-generated images. That is effect, not cause. The popular film industry makes optimistic films because most humans, like Claire, *already insist on seeing the world that way*. The illusions are within us: our blindness will not be avoided by putting away our bag of cinematic tricks. Indeed, we can perhaps use this bag of tricks to see as the werewolf sees. From this nighttime perspective, even Wagner's music, super-slow motion, and computer-generated images can be recruited into the project. Pessimistic popular film is hard to make because it is normally not pleasant to look at. It even requires us *to look at nothing*, like the black screen that persists for a long time in *Melancholia* after the destruction of the Earth and before the final credits.

Likewise, to be a self-acknowledged citizen of a world that contains evil is not an easy vocation. You will be perceived by others as alien or outlaw, as Justine is even by members of her own family. Representing evil in politics may require conjuring tricks, tricks of the imagination such as those called for by James and Kateb, and tricks similar or analogous to those von Trier uses to bring us closer to the werewolf's perspective. Confronting evil, especially in ourselves, is hard because it is not an object to be demolished but a darkness, or absence, from which, against all our instincts, we must not avert our eyes.

What would it mean to act as a pessimistic representative in democratic politics? First, it would mean that the representative act cannot simply consist in repeating, or even refining, that which citizens already say directly and openly. Not only do we often keep silent about that which we are ashamed, but we often do not see the evil within ourselves in the first place. Evil hides from view both in the sense that its perpetrators hide it and in the sense that even those perpetrators are not always capable of seeing what they truly are. For representation to add something valuable to political discourse, it must bring these things to light, even if it is unpopular or unpleasant to do so.

This suggests that such a representative must be prepared to endure the infamy that such an act often generates. And this in turn suggests why such representatives are few and far between. Truthful representation is not fidelity to what a population says, or thinks, or believes, but rather *fidelity to what they are in the whole, for better or worse.* I don't mean in the least that anyone is obliged to advocate for evil, but we are obliged not to pretend that it does not exist or to participate in a representation that suppresses its existence. Von Trier's films suggest that those who bring evil to light are soon identified with it, and it is easy enough to recognize that this happens in ordinary politics as well (e.g., most obviously, those exposing racism are often accused of fostering it or perpetuating it).

In Chapter 5, I will suggest that we cannot be satisfied with representation as the report of momentary preferences but, instead, should think in terms of the larger accumulation of personhood over time. Here, we must add that such an enlarged perspective is not simply the addition of many momentary preferences; it must include those things that the person would not, or cannot, report directly. Von Trier's evolution can illuminate what I mean. In the Dogma 95 documents, there is a certain affection for an unmodified democracy of moments—as if the director simply accumulates instants with his camera and makes no distinction between them or judgment on them. But the mature von Trier's films recognize that this is both an abdication of judgment and an impossible stance in the face of evil's tendency to retreat from view. Whether it is a single person or a people to be represented, a rounded representation may well reveal more than its subject would want.

We might want to think of such a representation as a higher kind of objectivity, but in fact, as James and Kateb remind us, it is really a deeper form of subjectivity that we are talking about. When von Trier wants to give us a view of the Earth, he does not employ a crowd of characters or a scientist; rather, he uses one woman, Justine, to deepen our understanding of an entire species. Representations are not necessarily improved by becoming more dispassionate, just as they are not improved by being naturalistic. Instead, they are improved, as James and Kateb suggest, when they reveal the depths of personality, even the ugly depths, that are often hidden from the light.

Still, we could draw the lesson from *Melancholia,* and even from *Europa,* that it is *possible* to be this kind of representative even in a world saturated with evil. Justine has the task of witnessing the world and representing it to others. Her presence and her actions bring to light what others would rather not see. She denounces the empty ambitions of her boss in the advertising agency. She disabuses her sister of her self-delusions. She even attempts to comfort her young nephew as the end approaches with an improvised ritual. It may not be much, but at least she models an unselfish, truthful approach to the world that is the direct opposite of the other characters, whose seeming generosity toward Justine is in fact predicated on a solipsistic and self-serving worldview (actually, a world-blindness). Justine brings truth and even "a little kindness" into the world in a way that her optimistic counterparts never do.

One might conclude that it would require a kind of saintliness to perform this sort of representative act, and indeed, von Trier has often been attracted to saintly heroines who are willing to take the sins of the world onto themselves, so to speak (*Breaking the Waves, Dancer in the Dark*). From a democratic perspective, however, we might equally say that the most effective representatives, like Abraham Lincoln and Nelson Mandela, have been those who are able to represent the whole polity, even those elements of it that they find hateful and evil and alien to themselves.

If such acts appear to be miraculous, they are certainly not feats of objectivity but, indeed, an achievement of a deep, subjective understanding of their nation and its evils.

Representation can improve on direct democracy not by filtering evil out of a population but, paradoxically, by accentuating it or, at least, by bringing it clearly into view and focusing our attention on it. Justine's actions will not redeem the world, but that would be asking too much. Is hers not a familiar situation to many of us? To find ourselves awash in evil that it is beyond our power to alter? The final words of the narrator of *Europa* are truthful and offer no comfort: "You want to wake up. To free yourself of the image of Europa. But it is not possible."

So long as evil persists in the world, we are condemned to represent it if we want that representation to contribute to our freedom. Cinema pessimism is one element of such a representation; political pessimism is another.

[5]

THE *UP* SERIES AND THE FUTURE OF REPRESENTATION

"It's not a picture of me, but it is a picture of somebody."

—*Nick, in* 56 Up

Are we in a golden age of representation? Though our initial instinct might be no, a strong case can be made for an affirmative answer. In politics, most Western countries have representative institutions that are, by some measures at least, extraordinarily responsive. Not only are elections broadly free and fair, but Internet communication allows elected representatives to stay in a high level of contact with their electorate in between elections. Reams of polling data can ascertain what the population thinks and believes on an endless variety of subjects. Email and social media that are nearly free and instantaneous means that a flood of information, requests, demands, and opinions reaches our representatives on a daily basis. If there ever were good excuses for being out of touch with one's electorate in the past, these have now largely been eradicated. While we worry about the corrupting effects of wealth, ideology, and power on our representatives, we take for granted this technological transformation that has brought constituents and representatives closer together than they have ever been before.

If all this is the case, then why do we remain so dissatisfied with representation and our representatives? Even as our political deputies struggle to keep up with our ever-changing attitudes, one prominent, and perhaps

Cinema Pessimism. Joshua Foa Dienstag, Oxford University Press (2020).

DOI: 10.1093/oso/9780190067717.001.0001

predominant, mood among both the American and European electorate is a profound dissatisfaction with our representative institutions. Whether one looks to the American "tea party" movement, the Trump election, or the reemergence of populist and neofascist parties in Europe, there can be little doubt that a segment, at least, of the population of most democracies has a deep antipathy to its own representatives, however "responsive" they may be.

In the aesthetic realm, things are perhaps more complicated, but many of the same, or parallel, advances could be said to apply. Film was once an expensive material made with industrial chemicals and precious metals that required labor-intensive and time-consuming processing to produce good images. Now, though, digital recording and the miniaturization of cameras as well as distribution channels like YouTube, Vimeo, and the Internet more generally means that many kinds of artistic representation have been radically (as we commonly say) "democratized." And while it used to require a significant amount of capital to make a high-quality, feature-length film—such that one normally needed the backing of a large corporation to do it—that is no longer the case. "Every man his (or her) own producer" is the motto of the digital age, and though cineplexes are still largely dominated by corporate products, the paths of entry into this system have radically multiplied.

Does the democratization of film and other visual representations, however, result in increased satisfaction with them? It would be foolish to attempt generalizations, but here too there are signs of the opposite effect. Traditional film and television viewership is down, although the multiple modes through which media can be accessed also mean that such viewership is harder to measure accurately.[1] The use of social media has become ubiquitous, but so have incessant complaints about it. At the very least, we can say that the pervasiveness of modern representational media has not provoked an outpouring of expressions of fulfillment.

A microcosm of this situation, in both its political and aesthetic aspects, can be found in the *Up* series of documentary films. It is the idea of this chapter that we can better understand the dissatisfaction with representation if we look more closely at this unique set of films. But we can also see in them the path to a different sort of representation, one better suited to our character as complex, social, time-bound beings. The *Up* series is no ordinary set of documentaries; it has acquired a distinctive structure over the fifty years of its existence.[2] Its participants have had an experience of representation with few parallels in art or politics, one in which the full trajectory of their lives has been made visible to themselves and to others. It is this rich, multilayered representation through time that seems to me worth emulating, even if it does not, and cannot, produce continuous satisfaction in its subjects.[3]

THE *UP* FILMS AND REPRESENTATION

Conceived as a political polemic, there is little artistry in the series of films that began in 1964 with *Seven Up!* The politics of its makers, initially at least, were pretty simple-minded. And yet a case can be made that this is the greatest series of documentary films we have ever had or are ever likely to have. The films have evolved into an eight-part documentary series that is still being added to. Starting at age seven and repeating every seven years, fourteen individuals from all walks of life in England have been interviewed over a period of, now, forty-nine years, and perhaps continuing indefinitely until their deaths. In no other set of films is so great a length of time spanned with actual purpose-shot footage, and nothing compares in its efforts to depict the development of individual, ordinary lives. *Boyhood* (2014), the only fiction film one could group with the *Up* series, pales by comparison. Although the films reveal much about the subjects, England, and the British class system, I will ignore most of this to focus on what I think are some larger questions—namely, what, if anything, the series teaches about the nature of representation more broadly.

The *Up* series, I say, is a magnificent failure. Certainly, it is a failure in the establishment of the political point that it wanted to make. But more important than this is the frustration that Nick, one of the most reflective subjects, expresses in his remark that begins this chapter: "It's not a picture of me, but it is a picture of somebody." He does not really utter this sentence as a complaint but simply as a description of what has occurred. In one sense, we might say, he has been about as well-represented as any human in the history of the film medium has ever been, yet his concern is that he has not been represented at all. It is in this way that I think his condition parallels that of the modern democratic citizen: extraordinarily well-represented in one sense but, at the same time, thoroughly alienated from the scheme of representation as it stands. Although ultimately, I believe, Nick's protest is not fully justified, it is important to understand, at the very least, why he makes it—and why we might as well were we in his position.

BACKGROUND

The film series had its start as a forty-minute, one-time segment of a long-running British news series called "World in Action."[4] For the first film, fourteen children from "startlingly different backgrounds" (as the narrator tells us), all seven years old, were interviewed and then brought together in London for a trip to the zoo and a party.[5] The voiceover makes the purpose of the program reasonably clear—"Why do we want to bring these children together? Because we want to catch a glimpse of Britain in the year 2000"—and then goes on to quote the Jesuit saying that is the touchstone for the entire series: "Give me a child until he is seven, and I will give you the man."

The children, only referred to by their first names in this and all subsequent films, are quizzed on a series of topics. They are asked their opinions about school, about money, about God, and about their own futures. In the first film, they are also asked about one another after their joint outing.

The opening shots in the film, which are of some children working their way *up* through a jungle-gym, telegraph the filmmakers' original intent: to document young children—the future leaders of England's various classes—as they are about to start their long climb *up* through society toward their expected destinations as "executives and shop stewards." A preoccupation with the rich and poor explains the skew in the original selection of children. Of the fourteen, ten are boys, and only four are girls. Only two of the fourteen are middle class. Five attend very elite boarding or pre-preparatory schools, and the other seven are poor, with six from London's East End and one from a farm in Yorkshire. There is only one non-white child—not surprisingly, one of the East Enders.

Seven Up! is thus a film about class and destiny. The rich children describe the schools that their parents have already set down as their expected trajectory, all the way through university, including the specific college at Oxford or Cambridge they plan to attend (trajectories that, the future films reveal, do come to pass, or nearly so, in many cases). The poor, by contrast, have no particular expectations about their future—when the interviewer asks Paul, in a children's home, about his plans, Paul replies, "What's 'university' mean?"

That the filmmakers perceive the two groups to have different destinies is not surprising. What is perhaps surprising is the cause they identify. Although the point of the film is to identify the class advantages of the rich, the filmmakers do not emphasize, as one might expect, money, access, or even the different curricula at the two sorts of schools that the children attend. Instead, the problem is identified as one of *freedom*—the poor have too much of it. By contrast, the gift of class that the rich receive is identified as *discipline*. Indeed, the narrator states quite confidently that "this distinction between freedom and discipline is the key to their whole future." We are now so used to the idea, via Foucault, of the poor as relentlessly conditioned by the disciplinary apparatus of the state that is interesting to find the original filmmakers of *Seven Up!* thought in just the opposite way—for them, discipline is a privilege of the rich, obtained largely in private institutions, while the poor, inhabiting loosely structured public institutions, are largely deprived of it. More important than the content they learn in school, the upper-class children have piano and ballet lessons and tutors. They also have the well-ordered hierarchy of the English prep schools, where teachers are supplemented by masters and masters are supplemented by "head boys" such that even at the age of seven, several of the rich students are already in charge of even younger students.

The poor, by contrast, have nothing but their freedom. While the prep school children are being marched through exercises, the poor "amuse themselves" (as the narrator puts it) on the playground during breaks and after school, and they are shown being rowdy, boisterous, and prone to fighting. Much is made of the fact that upper-class children report their bedtimes to be around seven o'clock, while the undisciplined working-class children stay up until ten or eleven. The rich children are hardly ever out of sight of some adult, while the poor ones, we are told, sometimes go to the movies by themselves!

A perceptive viewer might notice that the upper-class children look rather miserable in their ballet lessons and militarized drilling, but the narrator takes no notice of this at all. When the two sets of children mix, the filmmakers show the upper-class children scolding the working-class ones for their unruly behavior and, later, complaining about it to the camera. In short, for all its sympathy with the working-class children, *Seven Up!* laments the liberty that they are afforded. Its vision of equality is a world where all are afforded the virtues of discipline and the pathway it supposedly opens to college and career. Over time, the limitations of this perspective become clearer.

Even by the time of the second film (1970), this outright condemnation of freedom must have seemed embarrassing to the filmmakers, and it is never mentioned again in those terms. Indeed, over the course of the later films, the meaning of the touchstone phrase gets almost entirely turned around. While "Give me the child until seven . . ." is initially used as the Jesuits would have used it—to underline the value of rigorous discipline and early training into a rule-bound impersonal order—in later films it becomes a way to highlight the individuality of the participants. The chance remarks and personality quirks of their seven-year-old selves are used to predict their highly individual destinies with the frightening precision that only hindsight and selective editing can create.

Yet the perverse emphasis on the danger of freedom comes back to haunt the films in other ways. Most importantly, it haunts the filmmakers themselves by working against the thesis that birth and class are destiny. This thesis is slowly given up in the course of the films, but not without some difficulty, as the individual differences of the fourteen subjects gradually overwhelm the intentions of the filmmakers to present a stark dichotomy. The freedom of the East Enders is manifested in the much more wildly divergent lives that they lead, which are far more interesting in a narrative (and hence filmic) sense than the predictably dull career and family tracks of the wealthy. But even some of the rich kids turn out in surprising ways.

To put it bluntly, if class and discipline were really destiny, there would be little to film after the age of seven but the playing out of a predicted pattern. And this would be highly boring, perhaps even to the point of being unwatchable: without development, suspense, or surprise of any kind, there would be no audience for any representation, no matter how well-intentioned. The decision to continue the films is already a kind of concession that unpredictable freedom is of more narrative value than disciplined destiny. *21 Up* (1977) begins with the narrator asking broad questions about the subjects ("What are they doing now? How have they changed? What sort of people are they?") The narrator of *Seven Up!* claimed, in effect, to know the answers to these questions already—and it is only because the real answers are *not* entirely what was predicted that it is worthwhile to make the film.

At the very least, we might say, it is the tension between freedom and destiny, between known structure and unpredictable rupture, that makes for an arresting representation. But what does this mean to the subjects and viewers of such a representation?

THE DEFEAT OF INTENTIONS

The struggle between the filmmakers' original intentions and their subjects' freedom is most visible in the changing structure of the films themselves. *Seven Up!* begins and ends with the children at play in the zoo and an adventure playground, an easy symbol for the unstructured world full of obstacles that they will soon enter. In between, however, the film is organized by a series of subject questions. The children are contrasted in their answers: first, the rich describe their daily lives, and then the poor; next, the subject is changed to family, and then to religion, and so on. For each set of questions, the film is edited so that viewers see a contrast of perspective on each subject. Although some of the children talk about their individual circumstances, the point is to emphasize the group differences.

The second film, *7 Plus Seven* (1970), continues this structure.[6] It begins and ends, as almost all the films do, with the opening and closing clips from *Seven Up!*—the zoo and the playground. Once again, an authoritative narrator introduces the purpose of the film as providing a glimpse of the future and refers to the film as "an interim report." And the children continue to be arranged by class and presented as comprising two contrasting groups, with the two middle-class children forming an awkward set of outliers.

Already at this age, there are some problems as the children themselves begin to push back on their use as props in a cinematic lecture about class. This resistance is most pronounced among the rich children, who came off in the first film as spoiled, precocious, and privileged. John, always the most articulate, complains, "We're not necessarily typical examples . . . There's an attempt to typecast us." The poor children do not complain directly, but their lives have diverged more from the expected storyline than might have been imagined: one has emigrated to Australia, another has won a scholarship to a prestigious boarding school, and of those who stayed in the East End, one has gone to a higher-track grammar school that puts her on a more professional trajectory. Forced to make sense of these unique and unanticipated life paths, *7 Plus Seven* begins to waver between depicting its subjects as types and depicting them as individuals.

This struggle continues through *21 Up*, and in *28 Up* (1984), the class structuring of the film breaks down entirely. *21 Up* is the first film in which the full names of all fourteen subjects appear in the credits (within the film itself, the practice of only using first names continues). *21 Up* also breaks the classes up into smaller groups based more specifically on where they were raised such that rich and poor—still contrasted—are now grouped semi-geographically: as the Londoners, Liverpudlians, the rural subjects, etc. But in *28 Up*, the grouping of clips around topics or groups of people is entirely dispensed with. After a brief introduction, *and without any explanation or description of the change*, the film is divided into fourteen segments of roughly equal length, each focused on a single individual. Even the ones who declined to participate at this age (two of the upper-class boys) are profiled, and the film updates their circumstances via publically available materials.[7] This individualized treatment remains the norm thereafter.

Already in *21 Up*, the framing has been altered: the opening voiceover no longer describes them as future executives or shop stewards, but rather asks only the general questions noted earlier. The narration no longer hectors the viewer with prepackaged conclusions about its subjects: the narrator only introduces the project and provides some factual updates about the fourteen individuals. While not explicitly repudiating the previous films' polemical purpose, *21 Up*, early on, allows the participants to complain about it and offers no defense. Peter expresses the view that "[t]hey [the filmmakers] got their conclusions settled already." Nick says, "People read a significance into it [the films] that doesn't exist." And Neil goes so far as to say, "Everybody [in the films] has broken any class barriers that could possibly have existed, and therefore the film itself has possibly defeated its own object."

This last remark seems notably untrue in that, at this age, the class origin for each of the fourteen has still determined, to a large degree, their current status. It might be more correct to say instead that the filmmakers have begun to be defeated by their own *subjects*. Director Michael Apted's ability to depict his participants as class-determined is frustrated not so much by their changing circumstances but rather, we might say, by their subjectivity. Both in their plurality and in their determination to reject Apted's imposed narratives, the subjects of the film (no longer children after all) assert their independence from the roles in which the filmmakers has cast them—perhaps to his chagrin since he continues to pester them with questions (if not narration) designed to establish his perspective.

By *28 Up*, in structure at least, Apted seems to have nearly completely surrendered. There is no framing narration at all, and after a few seconds of old clips, the film launches into one man's story (Tony's) without explanation. The order in which the fourteen are presented tells no particular tale and seems to have been determined to spread out the narrative surprises in a smooth distribution. Apted seems to have given in almost entirely to his subjects' desire for self-presentation. Most of them are married or partnered, and nearly all are presented sharing camera time with their spouses, some of whom are even filmed separately. The film does not investigate the subjects' lives beyond interviewing them and filming them consensually in various contexts. Apted even negotiates with his subjects about what material will appear in the films *after* he has taped them, in part to guarantee their continuing participation.[8] This structure persists in all the films that follow.

Here, we are seeing something that hardly ever happens: the subjects of a documentary participating in and even, to an extent, controlling the circumstances of their own representation. Though documentary film normally presents images that are themselves unaltered, directors still possess enormous power to shape a story through the selection of what to film and, just as important, in the editing process and narration that provide the order and tone of presentation.

The first two *Up* films, by these criteria, are traditional documentaries in which a director displays his material to make a larger point. Although the subjects of the film may speak, they cannot be aware of the edited structure of the film as they are speaking (since it does not yet exist), so they cannot react to the structure, either to support it or to resist it.

In an iterated set of films like the *Up* series, however, the subjects of the films have the opportunity that ordinarily does not exist to resist the filmmakers' framing and editing before it actually happens. And here, it appears, they have succeeded—at least to a degree—gradually imposing their own individualized representational structure on the later films.

From a certain perspective, one might think that this makes the later *Up* films more representative than the earlier ones. While they all contain footage of the same people answering the same sorts of questions, the later films no longer serve the polemical purpose that the directors imposed on the earlier ones. The director's perspective remains, of course, but it is just one among others—and not necessarily the most powerful. The subjects not only speak but, to a much greater degree, control the setting of their speech and its context. They choose how to present themselves and whom to present themselves with, if anyone. Most importantly, the later films depict them as individuals first and as class-representatives only second, if at all.

And yet, curiously enough, the subjects of the *Up* films are *not* really satisfied by their collective defeat of the director's intention. This dissatisfaction is displayed in various ways: some decline to participate; others participate while repeatedly stating their distaste for the enterprise. Some participate but refuse to watch the films.[9] But even those who participate more willingly continue to complain, from time to time, that their representation is inadequate. Some attack Apted directly; others, as Nick's "picture" comment indicates, seem to feel that the film medium itself is at fault. Of course, they all remain the victims of editing and compression: they sit for hours of interviews, of which only a small fraction will be shown. But perhaps their uneasiness and complaints signal a different kind of representative wish, or a different understanding of representation entirely. Let us explore what this might be.

THE PROBLEM OF TIME AND ITS ALMOST CONQUEST

The film *21 Up* actually opens with an interesting scene that is not repeated in any of the others. The subjects are reunited in London and given a screening of the first two movies. When this third film was made (1977), the earlier films were not available on tape or disc (neither were yet widespread technologies). It may well be that this was the first time any of the participants had seen the films since their original broadcast. Some of them laugh, some hide their eyes, some look embarrassed, some look non-plussed—the results are not surprising, but the scene serves to introduce a theme that comes to dominate the films as they evolve: *reflection on the self over time*. The point of the films is no longer class difference, but the evolution of the self made visible through the accumulation of memories. The audience is no longer presented with individuals at any one point in time, but with several life stages laid out in sequence, legible in a way that individuals are usually only legible to themselves via memory.

In a perceptive review written after only five films had appeared, Roger Ebert wrote, "To look at these films, as I have every seven years, is to meditate on the astonishing fact that man is the only animal that knows it lives in time."[10] Although Apted has never again staged a collective screening for his subjects, he has, in effect, structured the films to stage one for the viewer. Rather than relying on the viewers to watch and remember the older films, the later films are designed to provide exactly this same experience to all those who watch them.

The later films, however, do not simply rely on the earlier ones to provide background or to catch the viewers up. Rather, they employ a kind of sedimentary approach, where each subject is introduced and displayed in a stage-by-stage way. Contemporary clips are layered on top of earlier ones so that what is presented is not so much the immediate views and perspective of the subject (though these naturally appear "on top," as it were) but their evolution through time. In some of the later films, perhaps up to seventy-five percent of what is shown is derived from earlier ones. And the films themselves naturally become longer as the layers pile up.

Reviewers often mistake, or misdescribe, this feature of the later films. Each release now provokes a round of reviews that usually note how, because of the use of accumulated footage, one doesn't have to see the earlier films to enjoy the most recent one. This is true enough, but the older clips are not just inserted as background knowledge for first-time viewers. Instead, the sedimented, sequential depiction of individuality has become the point of the later films and their main avenue of interest. Indeed, it is hard to see why a collection of interviews with fourteen (now thirteen) randomly collected forty-nine- or fifty-six-year-olds would be of much significance. What *is* of interest is something that can hardly ever be seen on film: the actual emergence of a real individual life over the course of half a century.

That this sedimentation is intentional is testified to by one formal quality. In *7 Plus Seven*, the footage from the first film was readily identifiable because it was black-and-white, while the contemporary footage was in color. In *21 Up*, Apted tinted the *Seven Up!* footage to further distinguish it. But starting with *28 Up*, all the footage is presented in whatever state it happens to be—that is, there is no longer any attempt to visually flag "background" from contemporary material. In practice, of course, differing film stock and quality, and the changing appearance of the participants, normally make a temporal location readily apparent to the viewer.[11] But the point is that no stage has any kind of formal priority—every moment contributes equally to the telling of the story of each life. So the time-consciousness that Ebert points to as an essential element of human life is reflected in the structure of the film.

Here, we touch on a quality of these films that exemplifies the larger promise of the film medium itself: the capacity to record duration. When photography first appeared, its ability to nearly replicate human vision had a revolutionary effect. Film promised to extend that revolution by making possible the sustained replication of vision through time. And so it does, but normally to a very limited degree. One can look at these limits in various ways. The average shot length in a contemporary Hollywood film is under five seconds.[12] Presumably, that figure for modern documentary film would be much longer. Even here, though, the shortness of any cinematic glimpse stands in contrast to the continuity of vision that we experience on a daily basis through our own eyes.

In addition, while in principle films themselves can be of any length, in practice our limited span of attention means almost all commercial films, even documentaries, are under three hours—and most under two. Exceptions, like Claude Lanzmann's eight-hour *Shoah*, are routinely described as "monumental" and require the excuse of an extraordinary subject. (Think about how strange this is: no one would describe a book that takes eight hours to read as "monumental.")

These two kinds of limitation are readily apparent, but it is another kind of limitation—one more rarely reflected upon—that most films, whether fiction or documentary, are shot and composed over a limited period of time. Even documentaries that use archival footage must normally be composed within some short period, normally no more than one or two years.

The rarity of the *Up* series, then, appears in its potential to defy this last kind of limitation. It suggests the potential for a kind of representation that is normally off-limits even to a medium, like film, with the capacity to record duration. As time-lapse films make visible to us normally imperceptible movement such as the growth of flowers or the motion of the sun, so do the *Up* films make it possible to see, in a way, the growth and development of individuals other than those we know personally. Indeed, through the compression of time made possible by edited sedimentation, these films, potentially, allow us to *see* that development in a way we cannot see even with members of our own family.

And yet here too the achievement of the *Up* series is also a marker of limitation. We do see the evolution of characters—some predictable, some utterly astonishing—in a way that hardly ever appears on film. But if the films succeed in overcoming one form of limitation, they remain bound by the other two: length-of-shot and length-of-film. Were they to attempt to defy these as well, they would begin to run up against a different kind of time-problem—a perfectly representative film would have to be as long, and as uninterrupted, as its subject. As one of the participants says, "we'd be on for months."[13]

Here, then, we get to some part of the continuing frustration of its subjects. On the one hand, the fourteen individuals are about as well-represented as we could imagine them being in this medium, or in any other. The whole length of their lives is faithfully covered, and they themselves are the principal narrators of it. They have been able to cast aside the ideological structure that was originally imposed on them and, to a large degree, craft their own account of themselves. Apted does not spy on them outside of scheduled interviews—almost everything we know about them, they themselves have told us, although if they told outright lies Apted could counter them, as he occasionally does when he thinks that they exaggerate or misdescribe. To the viewer, it appears about as intimate and honest a portrait of a self over time as we are ever likely to have.

Yet the subjects do not readily recognize themselves in their representations. They often use the later interviews to correct the misperceptions that they feel were introduced in the earlier ones, only to repeat the process at the next round. Nor do they necessarily feel the continuity of personality that the viewer perceives. "When you look at the seven-year-old us," says Sue in *49 Up* (2005), "it's difficult to believe that it is us; it's like it's someone else." What explains this persistent feeling?

There are at least two problems intersecting here. First, of course, is the problem of selective editing. Yet perhaps more important is a larger problem that we can all experience with our own old photos or home movies: the time-bound development of individuality, which we experience subjectively, is confronted in such cases with its static capture on film. And this can produce a feeling of disconnection even when the older images are perfectly unaltered and true. Any person, looking back over his or her life's actions (or old photos), will find some of these to be so alien to his or her contemporary self-understanding that they appear to belong to another person entirely, or to a persona so far in the past that it is hard to feel any connection to it. Neil, beset by mental illness, already expresses this problem at the age of twenty-one: "I find it quite hard to believe that I was ever like that [quite carefree and cheerful at seven] . . . but there's the evidence."

Neil's frustration here is *not* with the editing or the direction but really with the fact of representation itself, at least in this form. He does not contest the veracity of the images but instead questions their connection to his sense of self. Putting it another way, we could say that while they are truthful in their objectivity, the films cannot really account for the *subjective experience that is actually Neil's*. And although *we* might well trust the old footage over Neil's own recollections, that does not make it any less likely that, were we in a position equivalent to his, we would share his exact frustrations. Even if we do not contest the objective faithfulness of the film, we are in no position to defend its *subjective* faithfulness.

The nature of this dissatisfaction is perhaps most forcefully illustrated in an extended exchange between Apted and Jackie, one of the participants from the East End, in *49 Up*. Hers has been one of the most turbulent lives—after apparently rising out of poverty as a young woman, a series of failed relationships and illnesses have left her an unemployed single mother of three living off the generosity of her relatives and public assistance. She complains about the films rather bitterly to Apted, saying, "You will edit this program as you see fit," and, "This may be the first [film] that's about us rather than about your perception of us." But when Apted asks in reply, "How have I got you wrong?" and "So what do you want to talk about? If you would like me to represent you?," Jackie struggles for an answer.

After complaining a bit more about Apted's supposed misperceptions, she says, rather nebulously, that she wants to talk about "what I would like to do, what I hope to do." A little later, she adds, "I enjoy being me. But I don't think you ever really expected me to turn out the way I have." Although these remarks are vague, they seem to me to indicate a frustration with the fact that the films depict, as they must, what its participants *say* and *do* rather than what they *think* and *feel*—that is, *how they experience the world as subjects*. Jackie's complaint, although focused on Apted, is perhaps better directed at the medium of film itself, which though powerful can never penetrate beneath its object's surface.

Unlike a map, which renders a physical landscape as a physical replica, there is really no danger that film will ever perfectly represent its object—at least *not when its object is a subject*—for the subjectivity of persons, although a phenomenon of duration like film, is not a phenomenon of the same nature. Nick's complaint, that the *Up* films are a picture of "some-*body*," but not of him, seems exactly right. There will always be a distance between the body that appears on film and the self that exists as the experience of a person, even when the conditions for the representation of that person are nearly ideal, as they are in this series.

Yet we must also note that whatever limits the films have, they also give us a view of these individuals far richer than we could have by seeing and talking to them, even in person, at any one point in time. Through the time-layered portraits in which the later film have specialized, we get a rich, condensed account of these people that it is hard to imagine bettering within the medium. Reviews of the later films emphasize this while also describing them as powerful universal portrayals of human development, despite the relatively narrow backgrounds of the subjects.[14]

FREEDOM AND REPRESENTATION

Here, we might begin to turn back to the question about what it means for representation to succeed or fail in the political sphere as well as the aesthetic one. Early defenses of representation in politics, as I mentioned in Chapter 1, emphasized the physical barriers to direct democracy—the size of populations, the distances polities span, and so on. Later defenses were explicitly elitist, emphasizing the poor decision-making qualities of the unwashed masses. Neither sort of defense holds much water today: technology has defeated the first, and the human egalitarianism of the twentieth century has largely defeated the second.[15] If we are to tolerate representative institutions today, it must be on some other basis, just as representative plastic art has had to find another basis in the age of photography and video.

We can reconsider the tension between freedom and destiny, already visible in the first *Up* film, to address these questions. The filmmakers originally disparaged the freedom of the poor because it did not give them a clear path *up*—that is, it seemed to deprive them of the predictable narrative arc that they presumed all their subjects to *want*, if not at age seven, then soon, and for the rest of their lives.

Another way to say this might be that the filmmakers' outlook embodied a sort of optimism—not about the outcome of any particular life (indeed, they were very worried about the poor) but about the nature of life in general. A non-upward life was, to them, no life at all—worth recording only as a failure or a loss. Apted has maintained this view throughout his fifty years of interviewing, constantly asking his subjects whether they shouldn't have done more or better with their lives and questioning why they are satisfied with what appears to him to be mediocrity.[16]

It is, however, the great virtue of the film series (and perhaps of Apted as director, rather than as interviewer) that the individual diversity of the participants has persistently overwhelmed the narrow trajectory of success that cramped the vision of the early films. Freedom, it turns out, even when it leads to failure, makes for a better story than optimism. True freedom is unpredictable, and the unpredictable is especially worthy and capable of representation.

Freedom, indeed, calls out for representation in a way that a story predicted in advance does not. It is the unexpected qualities of what has happened to so many of the participants that have made the *Up* series such a success. The upper-class participants in the film have largely followed the path laid out for them from childhood. They have maintained their wealth and status and, for the most part, appear to be perfectly nice people. But their accounts are always the most boring, and it is only when they deviate from the golden path (Suzy drops out of school and goes to Paris; John reveals his status as the child of immigrants) that their stories seem worth paying attention to. The poor and middle-class children, by contrast, have led more varied and interesting lives. They have moved, emigrated, held a variety of jobs, come up and down in the world. *Their freedom*, in other words, though maligned by the original filmmakers, *has become the films' greatest subject.*

To apply this lesson in a political arena, we might say that the mere report of citizens' status and preferences is no longer something at which our elected representatives particularly excel. There are many electronic means, even in a large state, for ascertaining quickly what it is that people say they want at a given moment. Representing freedom, however, is a complicated task—and is more than a simple reflection of citizen preferences at any one time. Representing free citizens is difficult because of the inherently protean character of individual life; but it is an inherently worthwhile task.

The unpredictable and individual character of the *Up* citizens, even the rich ones, is not really depicted by their self-reports but in the sedimented cumulation of their lives. It emerges in the *totality* of the films rather than from their mouths. And it is the time-lapse quality of the films that allows it to emerge so vividly. The films, then, represent something real that nonetheless has a hard time presenting itself. We can see these individuals, imperfectly but still more completely than we could by meeting them in person. In a way, again imperfectly, we know them as we can know ourselves: as an accumulation of memories. Without denying their subjects legitimate frustrations, we can say that here, at least, is a situation where the act of representation participates in the revelation of a truth that is otherwise poorly visible. Here is a pessimistic cinema, and a form of representation, worth pursuing.

It is pessimistic because it refuses the preordained narrative arc of optimistic film and optimistic politics. In *Seven Up!*, the filmmakers presumed to know what would be best for all the children; the later films have given up that pretense, but not on the project of representation. This involves not only listening to the subjects but seeing the structure of their lives emerge over time. For a political representative to allow the freedom of his constituents to emerge from his or her work would thus require the same patient work of accumulation and editing that the filmmakers have undertaken in the *Up* films. Not every representative, of course, can embark on a fifty-year project of understanding before speaking. But the films at least offer us a vision of what a better kind of representation might entail: *a grasping and presentation of citizens as emergent in time and, thus, as more than what they say or do at any one moment.* I will have more to say about this in the next section.

If we believe the time-lapsed film is superior to the snapshot, however, we are also saying that we believe the cumulative representation is superior to the momentary report. Rather than reflecting the preferences of the instant, then, the representative can claim as his or her special task the detection and display of the free individuals that emerge over the stretch of time. Even in the simplest cases, this cannot be a matter of mere cumulation but of an edited perception—what we might call a curation of the whole. Perhaps we can even see the best speeches, for example, of a Nelson Mandela, or an Abraham Lincoln, or a Martin Luther King, Jr., as exemplifying such a process. Often against the immediate desires of their audiences, they gave an account of their communities' whole substance that was intended as a true reflection of its accumulated wisdom and meaning. Though sometimes perceived to be "ahead" of their audiences, in fact they spoke from an historical perspective that was intended to bind up the amassed, but disorganized, understanding of the many moments of their past. For this reason, we can see their words as representative even when not reflecting the immediate preferences of any member of their audience.

We do not need to believe, as earlier generations did, in the ignorance of the people or the wisdom of elites to believe that such a synthetic, curatorial process requires some kind of expertise that might be imparted by perspectives and experiences not everyone has the time, or the patience, to acquire. If we are to defend any kind of elected representation in an age of radically democratizing technology, this at least constitutes one possible path to do so. Such representation, it is safe to say, will never be commonplace or easy to accomplish, but understanding its nature can at least help us set a goal for those who attempt it. Every citizen can, and indeed should, speak for themselves. But that does not exclude the possibility that the freedom of every citizen might also be represented by another in a way that the citizen himself or herself does not have the perspective to achieve. Whether such efforts succeed is for every citizen to judge—both of representations of himself or herself and of others—as the subjects of the *Up* series judge of their own representations and those of their peers. Understanding the limits of their own representations may well color their judgments against such efforts—but understanding the *difficulty* of the *task* of representation might also tilt their judgments back to a greater degree of sympathy.

THE EMERGENCE OF INDIVIDUALITY

If Jackie and Nick's complaint about the failure of the film to reflect their subjective experience is one measure of the problem of representation, we cannot be satisfied with that as the only perspective on the representative act. Jackie's complaint, we might say, about the director Apted is that he doesn't really know her. But the *Up* films also show the reverse problem—the individuals on display, we repeatedly learn, *don't know themselves* either. Here, again, is a basis for thinking that the film can show us something of the individual that that individual is never quite in a position to show.

Throughout the various *Up* films, as the initial project of exhibiting the determination of class wore off, Apted, as director and editor, seems to have taken an increasing delight in showing how his participants' predictions about themselves are also wrong. Suzy is shown at age 21 saying how she won't get married and doesn't like children—then the film abruptly cuts to her holding her baby at 28. Symon at age 28 says that Yvonne is the only woman he could have married—but the next time he appears, he is married to someone else. Bruce at age 21 says he won't be a teacher, but then at 28 he is. And at 35 he seems a terminal bachelor and perhaps closeted, but then at 42 he is happily married. Most improbably, Neil, who is mentally ill and homeless at age 28 and predicts his own death, has become an elected Liberal Democrat town councilor at 42 and a lay pastor. In all these cases, Apted uses jump cuts to indicate the unpredictability of the changes, which are never fully explained, as well as how poorly the participants have anticipated their own futures.

The surprise of the unexpected future is a powerful indicator of the unknown substance of individuality—we are much more than our hopes and expectations, and it would be incredibly limiting if we were not capable of exceeding our own imaginations. If a representative cannot know us as we know ourselves subjectively, the representative can still have a kind of knowledge of these larger possibilities. The democracy of moments might speak more clearly through such a representative, speaking for many, than through any one voter speaking for himself or herself.

The surprise of the unexpected future is not the only kind revealed in these films. There is also an unexpected past—not something unknown but some part of the past that becomes newly meaningful as an individual life continues to evolve. One of the most remarkable features of the later films is the way in which contemporary events throw light or add significance to clips from the past that a faithful watcher of the series will have seen many times before. One of the most powerful examples of this is the story of John, who always appeared as the most urbane and polished of the public-school boys, possessed of an impeccable accent, a taste for hunting, and (by his own account) reactionary political views. He appeared, for the first four films, to fully embody the British upper class, the self-perpetuation of which the filmmakers were so intent to criticize. Then, in *35 Up* (1991), it is revealed for the first time that he is actually the son of Bulgarian immigrants, and in later films, he speaks about how his widowed mother worked to put him through boarding school and Oxford.

Not only does this come as a revelation to the viewer, who may have heretofore found John loathsome, it profoundly alters our view of all the earlier presentations of him. What looked before like an effortless exercise in privilege now looks—*without in any way being visually altered*—as a desperate attempt to fit in. When we actually hear John speaking Bulgarian, we realize that his posh British accent must in fact be something studied and practiced rather than a family inheritance. His expensive clothes now seem like a self-chosen costume rather than an expression of aristocratic privilege.

While John's Bulgarian identity was obviously never a secret to himself, it also seems clear that its meaning for him (and thus for the rest of us) was changed profoundly by external events. The fall of the Berlin Wall in 1989, which permitted a return to historic family property, as well as his marriage to a woman with Bulgarian ties changed the value of these elements of his past decades later. In the 1990s, he starts a charity for Bulgarian causes and devotes a great deal of time and money to it. He begins to spend more and more of his time there and to arrange for the care of Bulgarian orphans, something he has never done in Britain. So while John does not share the viewer's sense of total revelation, it seems completely correct to say that the events of middle age have thrown a new light on his earlier years, *even for him*, and have given them a weight and consequence they might not have ever had for him before.

While John's story is the most vivid dramatization of this retrospective projection of meaning onto the past, there are many others. Nick spends his early years trying to escape from the Yorkshire Dales only to grow increasingly attached to his identity as a "Dalesperson" as he ages in far-off Wisconsin. Symon names his last child, born when he is forty, after the father who abandoned him and about whom he never speaks. Even Tony's laments about the racial transformation of London's East End add an unthought-of dimension to earlier clips of his impoverished childhood there.

When Nietzsche wrote that "there is no way to tell what may yet become a part of history," he called attention to exactly this phenomenon: while the events of the past may be materially fixed, their meaning is always open to change because they take their meaning from their relationship with an ever-changing present.[17] As the individuals in these films pass through time, they change not only by acquiring new experiences but also through the effect that each stage exerts on the meaning of the past. Each film recaps its subjects' development, but even when the same clips are used, the recap seems a little different each time.

To say that a citizen's identity emerges over time, then, is not simply to say that people change as they get older. It is to say that their entire past may be changed in its meaning by later events. That this freedom is displayed equally by rich and poor in the *Up* films indicates that it is not a product of wealth, discipline, or the absence of these, but of something that can befall anyone, whether or not they wish it. Here too, then, we see the potential for representation to reveal something that individuals might not reveal, or might not even see, of themselves.

What does it mean to faithfully represent such an individual? Here too representation faces a challenge that cannot be answered by the direct report of a momentary preference, or even, I think, through a contemporaneous dialogue of individuals and representatives as imagined by some modern theories of representation (more on this in Chapter 6). If the individual that emerges through time is to be represented, it would ideally be through a mode of representation that allows each moment to speak as an equal to the others while understanding each not as independent but as related to one another, much as the different time-slices in an *Up* film are interconnected. As much as we obsess about the meaning of particular events when they happen, we must always reevaluate them in light of later ones. Representation must answer to the whole person, but the whole person is never fixed, even in the significance of their past. This is the extraordinary challenge that representing a free people poses.

This *tension* between freedom and its representation produces much of the drama, both in this film and in political institutions. To represent that drama is a skill, not easy to teach but perhaps easier to recognize. We do recognize great directors and political representatives, when they appear, which is not often enough.

PESSIMISTIC REPRESENTATION

> "Fail again. Fail better."
>
> —Samuel Beckett[18]

Early defenders of political representation in the seventeenth century expressed a kind of anxiety about the distance that would inevitably appear between a mobile population and a fixed set of representatives. *Corruption* was the word inevitably used to describe the actions of a faithless representative. Usually, this meant that the representative acted on self-interest as opposed to the public interest. But the anxiety could also refer simply to the gap that may always open up between a voting public and those whom the public has elected to speak for them. Rousseau, as I mentioned earlier in Chapter 2, went so far as to insist that freedom and representation were entirely incompatible. It was impossible, on his view, for one person to ever rightfully speak for another when such speech could lead to binding law.[19]

There is a parallel to the problem of corruption in the representative institution of film that the *Up* series makes plain. Even once the expectations of success and failure for the different classes are dispensed with, the filming of the subjects at seven-year intervals creates a representation that, like Rousseau's imaginary parliamentarians, increasingly becomes a prison to those represented as the temporal gap between them opens up. As the interview with Jackie in *49 Up* makes plain, the picture of her as an object, however honestly rendered, will always be at a distance from her being as a subject—and that gap will always be a source of frustration. But as John's story also shows, a represented individual cannot merely be described by his or her own subjective thoughts or feelings, and certainly not at any one point in time. The relationship between all our moments is not entirely under a person's control, and any attempt in the present to simply subdue or ignore the past may always be undone by future developments.

Political representatives can be perfectly faithful only so long as the people they are charged with speaking for do not change. Once the represented begin to move, the representative, through no fault of his or her own, begins to speak falsely. But such change is inevitable, so the causes of dissatisfaction lie as much in the population as in the officeholder. Or perhaps it would be better to say that the freedom of an individual, or of a people, is in inevitable conflict with any efforts at representation that can be made on their behalf. The representative need not be personally corrupt for the representation to be corrupted.

An officeholder who betrays his or her trust is simply dishonest. On the other hand, a changing population—or a changing person—is not dishonest at all but simply human. If human subjectivity is in time, then it is bound to change, so the difficulty of representing such subjectivity is primordial. Institutional arrangements can mitigate this problem, perhaps, but they cannot solve it. This is what it means to be pessimistic about representation. It must always fail, but some failures are better than others. When I said, therefore, at the beginning of this chapter, that the *Up* films are a magnificent failure, I meant that they have succeeded about as well as anything humanly possible.

The *Up* series is a portrait of freedom because it puts the protean element of human subjectivity on display as well as any film can. It is a failure of representation for the same reason. Again and again, the subjects of the series confront their earlier incarnations across the distance of time and find their representations wanting—both because they no longer resemble their earlier selves and because the film can never capture the interior mobility that is the source of each incarnation and each change. If the subjects were not free, there would be little or nothing in the later films that was not already in the earlier ones. So the films, much more than most, capture the tension between freedom and representation that every representative institution must experience.

Yet neither are the films themselves, with their sedimented display of individuality, a complete solution to the problem. Each film teaches us that the previous one was wrong in some crucial respects. With each film, we learn something new about the citizens that it represents, and not just because they have new experiences or have changed their mind about something. We are just as likely to reframe our understanding of what we saw in the earlier films as we are to see a new person—the presentation of the past is never fixed but emerges along with every new present.

If we are to have representative institutions, then we must attend to this tension and manage it. Representation, properly structured, may *express* freedom, but in its nature, it cannot really *embody* it. Rather, representation and freedom must always, in some sense, be at odds. Even if he drew his conclusions too extremely, Rousseau's instincts were correct about this much.

CODA

There is an irreducible poignancy about the *Up* series that this chapter has largely failed to describe. Although the lives depicted are prosaic, to see them captured as they are is almost ineffably sad. Perhaps it is the disappearance of potential over time as the limitless possibilities of childhood are reduced to the chosen paths of maturity. Even the most successful of the fourteen children have left something behind in their development, and when the road not taken is made visible, it produces a sensation of regret in the viewer, even if the subject feels none.

This is to say that as we are watching freedom appear in representative form, we are also watching it *disappear*. Every time we speak for another, we silence that person, if only for a moment. That is a burden that any honest elected representative will have to bear. It is not a job for the faint-hearted.

The *Up* series may fail at the task of representation, but perhaps each iteration of the film fails better than the last. Each one gives a fuller, richer portrait of its constituents, even as it produces new frustrations for them. It displays the freedom with which they live their lives and through which, purposefully or not, their individuality emerges.

If only our elected representatives could learn to fail better as well.

[6]

CONCLUSION

Cinema Pessimism

This book has explored two interrelated themes: the capacity of film to perform experiments in representation and the capacity of representation to perform democracy. Film is a modern medium, but so too is representative democracy a modern political phenomenon. Though they are hardly perfect analogues for one another, debates about both betray many of the same tensions, principally between, on the one hand, the ideal of mimesis and, on the other, the potential in representation for a creative, independent contribution to an ongoing conversation between the represented and the representative.

It is widely acknowledged that perfect mimesis is impossible: the Jorge Luis Borges story of the emperor whose map perfectly reflects his realm—but at the expense of duplicating it—is a tale that gets told in many guises to indicate the absurdity of such an enterprise.[1] Borges's very short story argues that this kind of mindless reflection should not even be a goal of representation: it should instead aim to emphasize, or distill, or beautify in a way that distinguishes the representation or the representative from the represented. Yet in popular discourse we routinely apply the test of mimetic faithfulness to our representatives and representations. Are my needs, goals, and identity perfectly reflected in that of my representative? Do they reflect the source accurately, honestly, and vividly? On the one hand, the goals of emphasis, distillation, insight, or beauty should allow the representation to achieve superiority to the represented. But the test of

Cinema Pessimism. Joshua Foa Dienstag, Oxford University Press (2020).

DOI: 10.1093/oso/9780190067717.001.0001

faithfulness implies a permanent flaw or inferiority of the representation, a standard that is ever unmet.

As our means of communication, both political and aesthetic, have developed across the centuries, this question has become all the more acute. Why have elected representatives at all when we could vote on everything directly via the Internet? Likewise, why have fiction film or painting when we can place a camera in every room of a house and view or broadcast the "reality" such cameras record? What do we want from representation in an age when certain kinds of automatic reproduction—and direct connection—have become routinely and cheaply available?

I have used the films discussed in this book to indicate the ways in which representation can (although it often does not) complement the unrepresented existence of the modern citizen with a perspective, or a vision, that adds something of value. At the same time, I have maintained there are dangers in representation for which its contemporary defenders in political theory have not fully accounted. The reader may be forgiven, at this point, for feeling like a tightrope walker that I have pushed and pulled in opposing directions without offering any bannister for support. That was, I confess, exactly my intention. But I hope it has been noticed as well that, as we have proceeded down the rope, so to speak, we have moved from films that are primarily warnings to those that articulate in a more positive way the possibilities available in different forms of representation. Here, I will try to jump out of the fighting line and, without resolving the paradoxes of representation or definitively characterizing its nature, express something of its potential value and meaning.

1

"I like to watch" is the iconic statement of a citizenry that has been narcoticized by representation. It is famously uttered, more than once, by Chance, the simple-minded gardener in *Being There* (1979), a film directed by Hal Ashby. Chance's thinking has been completely formed by television. He watches it indiscriminately, flipping constantly between cartoons, exercise shows, news, films, and whatever else is on. But this seeming variety of inputs and information have fostered no interests, thoughts, or cravings in him at all—other than the need to watch more. The joke of the movie is that Chance's fundamental passivity and lack of desire are constantly mistaken for maturity, restraint, and depth by the other characters so that, in a matter of days, he goes from penniless vagrant to potential President of the United States.

Released during a presidential campaign, the film was taken by many to be a critique of Ronald Reagan, whose sunny, dimwitted optimism Chance seemed to reflect. But the film is not a critique of Chance's character at all (in the final scene, he walks on water); instead, it is an indictment of the society that creates him as an empty vessel and then embraces that emptiness as heroic dignity. That is, the film encapsulates some part of the warning about the dangers of the representative condition for which Chapters 1 and 2 in this book attempt to argue.

From Chance's perspective, the world as he knows it is composed of little but representations. It is a pleasant environment—one he feels in complete mastery of via his remote control. Indeed, were he not removed from his Garden of Eden by unexpected events, he would never have known of his powerlessness (at first, he tries to escape danger by pushing a button on his remote). Even when confronted with (or enticed by) the real world, Chance only seeks to return to the enveloping comforts of television. His world of illusions has so thoroughly shaped him that when he encounters reality, he has no taste for it.

What is worse than Chance's inability to function as an active citizen, however, is the way in which everyone else treats him as a human ideal. These others have also been formed by our representative institutions, if not as completely as Chance. Even the most powerful among them lack the judgment or independence to perceive Chance's want of depth. Like a mirror (the simplest of all representors—the film is full of mirror references), Chance simply reflects back to them whatever they say and so entrances them. Complete narcissists all, they perceive themselves to be in a deep relationship with him, even though he is nearly incapable of any real human connection. As a single man, one passive citizen is hardly a threat to the republic, but in the land of the narcoticized, the sleepwalker may apparently be king. As in *Her* and *Blade Runner,* the ubiquity of representation helps everyone to mistake imitation for equality, and the result is a relationship of domination mistaken for one of freedom.

It is the optimist who thinks that pleasure and freedom naturally support one another or fit together neatly. In fact, the aesthetic and narcissistic pleasures of representation are, or can be, in tension with the equality and independence of a free citizenry. Pessimism, on the other hand, uses the working assumption that such tragic conflict is a recurrent condition in human history, one we can strive to lessen but not avoid. The pessimistic films that acknowledge this conflict may seem paradoxical—in condemning themselves, they seem to fall into performative contradiction—but the ones that fail to acknowledge the paradoxes of representation are, in a way, more dangerous. Whatever their subject, they preserve and forward the illusory comforts of a pacified existence that mistakes film content for independent experience. Such optimism, in fact, supports the disempowerment of citizens that critics of representation have always feared.

Individual films may be good or bad, both aesthetically and in the moral substance of their stories. We might even say that some of them promote justice or injustice, depending on that substance. But to ask whether justice inheres in the institution of cinema itself, or whether our culture is more just for being more cinematic, seems like a category mistake. It makes perfect sense, however, to ask whether we are more or less free, whether our society is more or less free, because of our participation in the institution of cinema, even if we are forced to answer largely in the negative when it comes to cinema as we have it today. That is the message of *Being There,* and the warning, at least, of *Her* and *Blade Runner.*

Yet we should not conclude this process of judgment too soon. Even more than representative democracy, cinema is still in its relative infancy. Although the *Up* films have reached the fifty-sixth year of their subjects lives and are already one of the longest projects of film representation in history, they could conceivably continue for another fifty years if they are to fully chronicle the entire span of those represented. "The best time to make up your mind about someone," it has been said, "is never."[2] And so may it be with institutions like cinema. Film is not done showing us what it is, and neither, perhaps, is representation more generally.

Time itself, or the time that it takes for a human to reveal themselves, is the central problem for both film and politics. Humans do not appear all at once, so we cannot ask them to *reappear* all at once either. A human being is something that makes itself available for presenting and representing only over time. That is why the *Up* series is more revealing of the humanity of its subjects, even more than most other films, which themselves already have the advantage over photography or portraiture of at least recording some extended duration. But if the *Up* films are some kind of improvement on normal film representation, it's not clear what kind of model they can be for political representation, which cannot wait decades for individuals or their representatives to speak. Politics requires decisions every day. What would it mean, then, for representation in general, and for film representation in particular, to serve rather than inhibit democracy and freedom? We can begin to answer this question by reviewing what some of the other films I have considered say about it. If we accept, as I have argued, that an eradicable tension exists between political representation and free individuals in the full exercise of their freedom and their individuality, what can we accomplish?

2

In the discussion of *Blade Runner* in Chapter 2, I insisted on the difference between mutual surveillance and mutual regard. They are both forms of living together, but in the first, we position ourselves as isolated beings taking stock of one another from a place of authority or pretended superiority. Surveillance, I claimed, can feel commanding and powerful, but it can also mask a reversal of power where what seems like a controlling audience becomes, itself, the object of control.

Mutual regard, as I described it, is not a substitute for representation. But it is a much better context in which representation could take place. Mutual regard refers to our recognition and enactment of human being as a condition that is continuously co-constituted by a collection of individuals. The characters of *Blade Runner*, whether biologically human or replicant, are not fully human until they acknowledge one another as such. As the protagonists shift from surveillance to regard, they begin to see possibilities in themselves, and in each other, that went unrecognized before. They bring each other out of the realm of objects, and into the realm of subjects, by sharing their subjectivity with one another.

One danger of representation—the danger represented by Samantha in *Her*—is that it tends to completely crowd out human relationships. But there is nothing inevitable about this process, no more than the pleasures of an unhealthy diet will necessarily crowd out sound nutrition. A society of mutual regard may require more self-conscious cultivation of its circumstances, as a healthy diet does, but that hardly makes it impossible to achieve. So the first thing to say about a freedom-serving representation is that it must promote, or at least inhibit as little as possible, the mutual regard that citizenship requires. Nothing is more important for this than the maintenance of social equality between citizens, including those citizens who may serve as representatives. While much recent attention has focused on the growth of economic inequality, the lesson of films like *Blade Runner* and *Her* is that social isolation is as much an enemy of equality as disparities of wealth. The spontaneous back-and-forth of genuine conversation is something both naturally human and yet increasingly hard to achieve in modern society, for the rich and powerful no less than for the weak and poor.

While this is not the place to propose specific policies to bring about mutual regard, it is important to note that this is as much a practice as a set of ideas. Mutual respect, by contrast (an idea, or set of ideas much promoted by political liberalism), is really just a set of individuals holding the same set of ideas. But mutual regard is a practice of paying attention to one another that cannot be done by anyone in isolation. Like Rousseau's general will, it is either something that some group creates together, or it is nothing. Nor can it take place in a single moment. Since humans unfold over time (*unlike* Rousseau's general will), mutual regard must take place over some length of time as well. So the good representative must foster this activity and the social conditions that make it possible, both those that promote equality and those that diminish isolation. Yet neither the space nor the time of mutual regard can be infinite; as a shared activity, it can only be shared by some finite number of people in an actual time and place.

Yet how can these boundaries of space and time be established or tolerated? In Chapter 3, *The Man Who Shot Liberty Valance* provided some grounds for addressing this issue. The problem the characters in that film face appears to be geographical: how to establish the boundaries of a constituency and the right to be a member of it. But their solution is as much temporal as it is topographical: borders are established not through drawing a line in the desert sand, but by the forging of a community of ongoing commitment to one another.

Although symbolized by the union of Ransom and Hallie, the state that their marriage stabilizes is not simply the heterosexual, patriarchal family writ large. For one thing, it includes the third character in their erotic triangle, Tom Doniphon, whose presence lingers in their relationship and creates queer connections, obligations, and sacrifice for both of them. But more than that, they are both bonded to the larger community that supports them and that they love in return. Their mutual regard is not merely inward, looking toward each other, but outward, looking toward their fellow citizens.

Not all are included in this state; it is in fact founded on the exclusion of the uncontrollable Liberty Valance. Although Valance's violence would be a problem for any state, I suggest that what really makes his citizenship an impossibility is his refusal to recognize anyone as his equal. Violent citizens can be imprisoned, but Valance's inability to engage with his fellow humans in any posture other than one of dominance makes him incapable of participating in mutual regard. Though he runs for the post of representative, as Ransom does, it is perfectly obvious to all that he will pay no heed whatsoever to his fellow citizens were he to occupy the position.

The representation that Ransom offers, by contrast, is not exactly selfless (he becomes famous and perhaps wealthy), but it does involve a sacrifice of self that ultimately neither Liberty, nor Tom, nor most of the townspeople want to make. In speaking for others, Ransom gives up something of himself (symbolized both by his nameless moniker and his childless marriage). And this is just why the community trusts him, and is right to do so, over others who claims to speak in their name. What cements mutual regard over time, then, is again not some set of ideas but an erotic bond that is long-lasting yet cannot be universal, either through space or through time.

The good representative is not an ordinary citizen, but neither is she or he extraordinarily knowledgeable or virtuous. Such a person, this film seems to suggest, is a willing hostage of some particular community, held in place by the person's love and sense of obligation to that community. In return for a privileged position and voice, the representative accepts a certain diminishment and loss of authenticity that most citizens do not. To the cynical eye, this can appear as hypocrisy when in fact it is a sacrifice. No doubt in practice it may not be so easy to tell the genuine representatives from the pious-sounding hypocrites, but in principle the difference should be clear. The freedom that the true representative supports always comes with a price. Anyone who evades the price for being a representative is not doing it right.

Speaking for others is, or ought to be, profoundly difficult. Because humans emerge through time, the representative is always trailing behind the constituency. This is not a deficit that can be made up by more or better polling. Speaking for another who travels from birth to death means carrying the burden of death that all reckon with, even if they do not recognize it all the time. Ransom Stoddard transforms from a person who carries law books to one who carries the responsibility for the death of another, and for making that death a tolerable cost by using it to create a democratic community. The good representative must carry the burdens of temporality for others and not let them get in the way of human society and reciprocity, as they could easily do.

Even *Liberty Valance*, however, does not reckon fully with what I consider one of the deepest challenges to any account of representation and the final reason we cannot be optimistic about its success: the persistence of evil within the human community. By depicting the character Liberty Valance as an animal, the film allows us to imagine that perhaps only the extraordinary or non-human needs to be excluded in order to a have a community of good citizens. *Melancholia* challenges this thought as it challenges many of our preconceptions about representation, filmic and political. Both *Melancholia* and *Europa* are concerned with a self-induced blindness in humans that can result in seemingly invisible evil permeating our institutions. Representative government, after all, has produced fascism as well as democracy.

In *Melancholia,* as I argued in Chapter 4, director Lars von Trier seems to ask us to see the world as a werewolf does—that is, in two distinct ways: the daytime way, which we might liken to the happy Hollywood version of reality, and the nighttime way, in which the permanence of evil is fully acknowledged. Since evil either hides itself or is naturally hard for humans to see, this second sight is an especially cinematic one, full of artistic flourishes. But it is nonetheless more realistic (to use an overused word) simply in the sense that it makes visible elements of the world, and of other people, that we normally hide from or allow to be hidden from us. Von Trier's seeming sympathy for Nazis, witches, and werewolves is not actually an appreciation of their character but more an acknowledgement that through them, we can see this hidden view of world.

Any honest representation of the world should not avoid this evil. This, I think, was at the core of von Trier's complaints about "bourgeois" cinema in the Dogma 95 documents. Whether or not I am correct about that movement, though, the problem of evil clearly poses a fundamental challenge to the potential representative. Is it not the case that representing evil is a form of participation in it? And that to represent evil *well* is to participate even more fully? How can a representative or representation avoid such a contamination?

I believe they cannot. Even more than Ransom Stoddard realized, I think, the role of representative is burdened by the service it provides to evil, and to evade that service is to fail as a representative. That is one more paradox we can add to the long list of paradoxes that Hannah Pitkin gave us about the representative situation. Along with inequality and isolation, a community of mutual regard is also threatened, permanently, by the evils of the world, including that inside each of us. One doesn't have to believe in a metaphysical evil to think there is something wrong with the perspective that always tries to see the best in people and ends up blinding itself in the process.

The representation of evil is a bitter and infamous task, and one not likely to improve the popularity of whomever carries it out. One of the greatest obstacles, then, to honest and complete representation is that it is not, in the end, what most people *want,* regardless of whether they admit it. It would require exceptional bravery to do it, and neither most filmmakers nor most elected officials are notably brave. Both professions, in fact, are filled with those seeking popularity. So such whole and truthful representation is bound to be rare indeed. It is up to us to recognize it when it occurs. To recognize that selfishness and sadism are a routine occurrence in human beings is not to celebrate them, but we cannot grapple with these old enemies of equality and reciprocity without acknowledging them. The good representative must do this as well.

Cinema pessimism thus comprises a set of overlapping concerns about film and democracy. First, that most popular film today, in perpetuating a false optimism, contributes to our social and political isolation and, thus, ends up undermining our democratic institutions. Second, that ideal representation is itself a painful, costly, and thankless task and, therefore, is unlikely to be stably present in any society, much less a democratic one. Third, that even the best representations and representatives are haunted by paradoxes and evils that they cannot subdue. If humanity in its great complexity is to be well-represented, then evil as well as good will speak through that process. Yet I repeat again that cinema pessimism is not hopelessness or resignation; it is a sober recognition of the limits of our institutions and a critique of the optimism available in both some democratic theory and some Hollywood cinema, which expect the task of representation to issue in a happy ending. For what kind of representation, then, can we pessimistically hope?

3

Being There has a certain Heideggerian tone. In fact, Jerzy Kosinski, the author of both the 1970 original novel and the screenplay, had *Dasein* (a key philosophical term for Martin Heidegger that could be translated as "being there") as a working title. Heidegger's critique of modernity centered on technology, or rather on the way in which modern technology rested on a larger instrumentalization of the world. To his way of thinking, it is not the machines themselves that are dangerous but the very idea that the world exists to serve us, causing us to view that world as a set of potential instruments and resources rather than letting it come into view on its own terms.[3] In a way, this critique is an echo of Rousseau's complaint about political representation, at the heart of which was a concern that when some humans come to serve others, the essential equality of a free relationship is lost.

There can be no doubt that film is a technology, or a set of technologies, making it, of all the arts, uniquely susceptible to this Heideggerian critique. And certainly, this form of condemnation has been made by earlier generations of film critics.[4] But if film is a technology, it is not *only* technology. The category of technology does not exhaust its nature. Especially in its representativeness, film is continuous with earlier arts, like the theatre, that require no technology at all. If film has displaced live theatre and opera as forms of entertainment, one reason is surely that it performs some of the same functions in a way that is similar enough to be an adequate (or superior) substitute for many audiences.

While Heidegger, like Rousseau, often lapsed into a romanticism that denigrated all representation, his student Hans-Georg Gadamer took another path. "The world that appears in the play of presentation," he wrote, "does not stand like a copy next to the real world, but is that world in the heightened truth of its being."[5] This means that when representation succeeds, it succeeds not because it reproduces the world as it already exists, but rather that representation can cause some part of the world to come to the fore and be visible in a way that it was not before. Or perhaps that something which exists only potentially in the everyday world finally comes to actuality in a work of representation. That is a characterization that can cover politics as well as it covers art. When we say that we see the best of ourselves in some work or representative, we mean that we see something we believe is really there, in some or in all of us, finally come to light in the shape of one work or one person. It is not something new, then, but it is newly out in the open.

Although film may be a new sort of art, it need not be something added on top of the world, like a coat of paint. When done right, it is, or can be, an elemental way of making the world visible. Hence, Gadamer writes of "the ontological interwovenness of original and reproduction," where the two are just differently visible sides of the same object.[6] The human world, he seems to think, does not fully exist until it has a chance to show itself in reproduction: "in presentation, the presence of what is presented reaches its consummation."[7] This sounds more opaque than it has to. It only means that if you think *56 Up* (2012), or any film or representation, reveals more about its subjects (and, perhaps, about you) than they themselves could tell you directly, you may not be wrong. When citizens recognize themselves in a film, or in a political figure (whether Barack Obama or Donald Trump), it means that that image or person speaks for them in a way that they can acknowledge even when it exceeds what they themselves can say.

No doubt this is an idealization and not what happens in every movie or representative act, or even in most of them. Nor does Gadamer take proper account of the political dangers that lurk in representation. Still, he expresses here a possibility for a productive kind of representation that is anchored in what it presents and yet adds something to it without duplicating it—an "increase in being," as he says.[8] Or, to put it more in the vocabulary of cinema pessimism, what he describes (too optimistically) is the impossible destination toward which we fail: a representation that increases the visibility of what we humanly are, both without getting in the way of it and without adding something false on top of it. Although Gadamer was no particular fan of the film medium, we can still see that its particular form of temporality offers, in the right circumstances, a special opportunity for the display of the human.

In the *Up* series, we saw the fundamental problems that time and subjectivity create for the project of representation as well as an imperfect solution to those problems. Human beings are hard to represent, not only because they are incredibly diverse but also because, even as single individuals, their unpredictable patterns of growth and change, along with the deep interiority of their experiences, make it impossible for any representation to keep up with its subjects. That is, because we really are free and really do change, representation is an enormous challenge. At the same time, this is exactly what makes representation worthwhile. If our interests were fixed and easily known, they could easily be communicated directly.

Individuals emerge through time. Such individuals are not readily known by others, or even by themselves. In that sense, they are fundamentally different from lifeless objects, and the nature of their representation must likewise be different. To fail better, in this context, means to come closer to the mark of displaying what is important to the fluid nature of such an unperfected, unperfectible creature.

The reciprocal equality that democracy demands as its best context is inherently unstable because the individuals who participate in it are always changing. A representation that succeeds in this context is one that perpetuates such equality instead of interrupting it. Such a representation, rare as it may be, furthers the back-and-forth of conversational exchange and, thus, contributes to political equality rather than undermining it. A lifeless copy of the world is just another object in service (and like Borges's map, perfect mimesis makes a perfectly useless object). But when representation helps the ever-changing citizenry to more easily or more clearly appear, it serves the purpose of promoting citizen activity rather than holding citizens transfixed and passive.

We can never be done with representing such creatures for the same reasons that we can never be done with making up our minds about them. Perhaps most representations today, and most representatives, attempt to short-circuit this process. In so doing, they contribute to the deadening of politics that critics of representation have long complained of. For representation to enable and energize democratic politics, it has to perform this revelatory function that it always has the potential for but rarely succeeds in consummating.

In the *Up* films, we get some sense of what this would look like. Truth and beauty are not beside the point, but for a representation to serve a democratic political function, these potentials must be sublimated into a presencing that makes us witness to something we can acknowledge as a new face of an existing body. We have all seen this happen enough to know that it is possible. And we all know it is rare enough to seem miraculous when it happens. To live in a representative democracy, we must make it our goal to bring it about more often, in whatever medium we can. Of course, a good representative will serve the interests of his or her constituency, but it is important to understand, at the same time, the emergent fluidity of those interests as well as the continuous need to preserve the ocean of mutual regard from which they emerge.

Just as diaries may make it possible for their authors to know themselves better by reflecting on their development over time, so the *Up* films help a community to know itself better, and to see itself as more than a collection of individuals, by making its own development over time visible. In this same way, we can imagine our political representatives in that role of making each part, and each time, of a community visible to the others so that all can get a better sense of the whole, and not just the current whole but the whole as a collection of beings that evolve over time. Thus, a good representative must remember the past and anticipate the future even when those present forget to do so.

It may seem frustrating at times that we do not elect our representatives all at once, or that they do not respond to our immediate preferences and desires once elected. But in fact, the view of representation elaborated here sees it as a virtue of the process when elections are staggered in time and a benefit that representatives are not subject to immediate recall. *Since human beings present themselves over time, they can only be re-presented over time as well.* That is why film has something to teach us about political representation, and why one of the things it teaches us is that what look like barriers to immediacy may in fact be enablers of human presentation.

This is not the place for a wholesale evaluation of potential arrangements of representative electoral systems. My aim here is only to develop the terms for such an evaluation, emphasizing the obstacles that are often overlooked to a representation that truly frees and empowers. But traditional questions of constituency size and shape, terms of office, qualifications for office, voting systems, rotation, and parties all look slightly different when viewed from the pessimistic perspective. Good representatives are not those with the shortest terms of office, the most communication with their electorate, or the most consistent voting record. The best representation would be one that displayed the fullest diversity of its representees in the whole arc of their lives, from past to present and future. It would be like a cubist painting where the different perspectives framed on a single canvas referenced different temporal frames as well as different spatial ones.

The more general challenge in creating a community of regard, rather than one of surveillance, is the fact that a system of election creates a set of snapshots of the community at single points in time, whereas the human lives to be represented take a time-bound, narrative form that is poorly represented by any snapshot, or even a set of them. That is why we appreciate representatives who can tell a coherent story about the people that they represent, one that sounds to them like an authentic account of who they are, even if the words are new to them. This too rarely happens, but without fail, we know it when it occurs.

Just because it unfolds over time, a human life, we can say, faces a necessary tension between a democracy of moments (in which each moment is as valuable as any other) and a lawful life of meaning and purpose (in which we sacrifice some moments in the name of others and justify these choices by reference to some meaning, norm, or story). Likewise, any representation of such a life faces a tension between the individuality, diversity, and chaos among the people to be represented and the coherent political life that they could share together. The latter is the implicit possibility that is only brought into existence by a successful representation of the former. Since the best films carry out a parallel task, they both show us the obstacles to this task as well as tempt us with visions of its success.

The best representative, then, brings to presence the whole community, past and present and future, good and evil, and creates the potential for all individuals to increase their self-knowledge—by increasing their knowledge of their emergent humanity in relation to the being of others. Or put another way: if we become more fully human by way of reciprocal relations with others, then a representative can be a lens that allows this fact to come into focus.

The new defenders of representative democracy in political theory, then, are right about this much: representative democracy *could be* the better sort of democracy if these conditions were to come about. And our films, likewise, *could* serve this end as well. Currently, though, our representatives, and our system of representation, is too geared toward the mimetic ideal to serve this purpose very often. And when we celebrate the success of mimesis (as in the hoopla around *Black Panther* and *Crazy Rich Asians* or the mere fact of Barack Obama's election), we set up a bad standard for future representative acts. No one is well-served (or has ever been well-served) by a representative who simply reproduced his or her immediate preferences or self-perceived identity.

We will only be well-served by representatives who attempt the difficult task of helping a whole polity of humans, in their extended plurality and totality, to self-knowledge and then self-enactment. While they will inevitably fail at this task, because the task itself is endless, some may fail better than others. And their failure might set an example for other, better failures in the future. Pessimism of this sort is not despair about the future but encouragement to meet its challenges within the limits of the human condition. That is the representation that enables freedom rather than supplanting it. I have, in this book, listed some of the films that I think meet this standard. Rather than listing the humans as well, I simply invite my readers to remember those who they believe have done so—and then to reflect on how short a list it is.

4

A final note for those still puzzled about the nature of the dual inquiry pursued here, and about the epistemological or ontological status I mean to assign to the films studied. Earlier, I described the films investigated in this book as experiments in the representative condition. By now, the reader will, I hope, have a better understanding of what I meant by this phrase. But how I intend these experiments to connect to more traditional approaches to political theory may still be a question. Originally, many texts of political theory would base themselves on historical examples. Indeed, theorists like Machiavelli and Montesquieu took it as their primary task to catalogue the possibilities of politics through the accumulation of historical events, just as a medical or legal text develops knowledge by generalizing from past cases.[9]

Yet political theory (even that of Machiavelli and Montesquieu) often contains a utopian or aspirational element as well. We could call this fictional element a projection into the future of a not-yet-realized possibility for human relations. It embodies a potentiality that is yet to emerge into history but that will be recognizably human if it does.

The films described in this book can be said to serve the same sort of function—of bringing a yet-unrealized human potential to light—but perhaps with a different emphasis. Often focused on the erotic, emotional, and visceral scenes of human exchange, these films give us a window onto the irrational elements of politics that traditional texts sometimes found hard to depict. In *The Man Who Shot Liberty Valance*, for example, we see the complex interplay of reason and desire, cemented by acts of violence, that constitute the founding of a state. The film's claim to relevance is not that real events are depicted, but that the interaction of emotions and reasons is a plausible revelation of what humans either could do or have, in some sense, already accomplished. This is a version (and a vision) of social self-constitution no more or less fictional than the social contracts of Hobbes or Locke. It represents not a factual truth but a human potential, the presence of which we sense but find hard to articulate. Even von Trier's depictions of human evil, though nothing a sane person would seek to imitate, tell us something true about the human world from which all politics must take its shape.

To take examples only from history, as Machiavelli and Montesquieu sometimes seemed to recommend in their methodological passages, is to confine one's political imagination only to what has occurred so far. But the protean character of human beings means that any fair representation of them must attempt to look beyond their past and into their future potential as well. Human beings are not chemicals whose reactive potentials can be fully known or calculated in advance. It is an old saw about science-fiction films that they are always about the present. One could just as well say that all political theory is about a future that is yet to be. To truly grasp the potentialities of human politics, and to have any hope of profitable instruction for its participants, we must retain a critical perspective on its history while simultaneously allowing our imagination to grasp the full range of examples available, including those examples of the imagined future that film can give us.

Liberation from realism and mimesis, we might say, is both practical and necessary if we are not to be imprisoned by the past. If any theory exists in relation to some set of examples, then the widening of that set must broaden the choices available to the thinker. If the genre of political theory is understood as that of a fiction-that-might-become-fact, then it is a genre that can include some films, as it already includes some plays and novels, alongside the most venerable treatises, essays, and books of the field. This book has attempted to promote such an inclusion. I leave it to others to widen the field further and in other, better dimensions.

NOTES

Introduction

1. See, for example, Eisenstein 2004, Kracauer 1960, Bazin 1967 and 1971, Baudry 2004, Benjamin 1968, Mulvey 1975, Deleuze 1986 and 1989, Cavell 1971 and 1981, Panagia 2013.
2. See, for example, Plato 1968, Book 2; Aristotle 1958, ch. 9; Rousseau 1960. See also, for example, Kant 2000, Schiller 1954.
3. See Cavell 2004, Deleuze 1986 and 1989, Connolly 2002a and 2002b. The phrase is from Deleuze 1989, 182.
4. See Mulvey 1975, Baudry 2004, as well as classic essays like Comolli and Narboni 2004 and Wollen 1972. See Rodowick 1994 for an excellent survey of this literature.
5. There are, of course, writers like Alain Badiou who reject the idea that film is, in fact, a representative art, but I do not find these claims (or their purported derivation from Deleuze) persuasive and do not pursue them here. See Badiou 2013, 222ff.
6. There is an enormous literature on *Blade Runner*, and it has certainly touched on this idea (e.g., Wilson 2005). See Chapter 2 for a fuller discussion.
7. See Francavilla 1991.
8. See Hobbes 1991, ch. 16–18. In Book II of *The Social Contract*, Rousseau responds that "sovereignty, being nothing less than the exercise of the general will, can never be alienated, and . . . the sovereign cannot be represented except by himself" (1968, 69).
9. See Frank 2010.

10. See Almond and Verba 1963 for the classic statement of democratic apathy. For the participatory response, see Pateman 1976, Macpherson 1977, Wolin 2008.
11. See Ranciere 2006, ch. 3.
12. See Tormey 2015 for a summary and further instance of this literature.
13. See Plotke 1997, Mansbridge 2003, 2009, 2011, and 2017; Urbinati 2006; Garsten 2010; and for a wider range of views, Alonso, Keane, and Merkel 2011, an excellent edited volume. Of course, this view is not without antecedents. Urbinati 2006 gives an excellent account of this history, citing in particular Paine, Kant, and Condorcet for a defense of the epistemic superiority of indirect democracy. Despite this history, I still think it is correct to say that the defense of representative democracy has become more vigorous and conceptually coherent in the last twenty years. Plotke 1997 gives some reasons for this. See Pitkin 1967 and Schwartz 1988 for the evolution of the concept of representation in political contexts.
14. See Williams 1998, Disch 2011, 2012a and 2012b, Saward 2010. See also Rehfeld 2005 for an attempt to isolate the virtues of representation from contemporary practices and Dovi 2012 for an attempt to identify the properties of a good democratic representative.
15. See Urbinati and Warren 2008 for an excellent historical review of the subject and Disch, van de Sande, and Urbinati 2019 for recent developments.
16. For critics of film representation, see, for example, Mulvey 1975, Metz 1977, Comolli and Narboni 2004.
17. Connolly 2002a and 2002b; Panagia 2013.
18. Honig 2015.
19. Some representative headlines: "The Provocation and Power of *Black Panther*" (*The Atlantic*, 2/14/2018); "'Black Panther,' 'Crazy Rich Asians' Success Changing Diversity Story" (*The Hollywood Reporter*, 2/9/2019); "Black Panther Is a Gorgeous, Groundbreaking Celebration of Black Culture" (*Vox*, 2/23/2018); "Diversity Wins in 2018: 'Black Panther', 'Crazy Rich Asians' and Midterm Elections" (www.kare11.com, 12/19, 2018); "'It's Not a Movie, It's a Movement': Crazy Rich Asians Takes on Hollywood" (*The Guardian*, 8/11, 2018).
20. See Urbinati 2006, Runciman 2007, Saward 2010, Disch 2016, Rehfeld 2018.
21. Pitkin 1967, 10–11. See Dovi 2015.
22. Plato 1968, Aristotle 1958, Ankersmit 1996.
23. Connolly 2002b, 12; Panagia 2013, 2–3; for a sampling of film materialism, see Barrett and Bolt 2012.
24. Baudry 2004, Benjamin 1968.
25. Mulvey 1975, de Lauretis 1984. See also Erens 1990.
26. Cavell 1971, Deleuze 1986.
27. On the first point, see Honig 2013; on the latter, see Anker 2014.

28. As a general matter, I would say that most commercial films are the product of a large collectivity (actors, cinematographers, costumers, directors, editors, musicians, screenwriters, set decorators, etc.) and, therefore, that to speak of the "intentions" of a film or a filmmaker is often a dangerous metaphor. Still, there is no general difficulty in speaking of the meaning of such a film or some part of it—as in any collectively authored work, meaning arises from the expressed text or image, however authored, in interaction with the context and understandings of its audience through whatever language they share.

    In some cases, however, a particular director or screenwriter (and especially when they are the same person) may have an outsize effect on a film. Several of the films discussed in this book fall into this category, so I will sometimes refer to them as if they were the work of these individuals. In doing so, I do not mean to be claiming that these films escape the general conditions set out in the previous paragraph. I merely use a common shorthand that seems justified in these particular cases.
29. Dienstag 2006.
30. That nature, physics, and biology also constrain our actions is certainly the case, but since these constraints arise irrespective of our political conditions, I do not consider them to be constraints on *freedom* per se.
31. It is here that the works of Stanley Cavell make their greatest contribution. Particularly in *Pursuits of Happiness* (1981) and *Cities of Words* (2004), Cavell describes the ways in which interaction with certain films (not all) can enhance our self-knowledge in distinctive ways. As I argue in *Cinema, Democracy, and Perfectionism* (2016), however, he does not take up the equally important question of self-enactment and, therefore, misses some of the ways in which the institution of cinema could be said to inhibit our freedom.
32. I take this to be a conventional position in the history of political thought, available, in different forms, in Aristotle, Rousseau, Hegel, and Arendt. My particular understanding of this condition will become evident in the chapters to follow.
33. A point well-made, in a different way, by Anker 2014.
34. This perspective is perhaps best typified by Rehfeld 2005, but it is certainly shared by many earlier contributions, including those of Schwartz and Mansbridge.
35. Schopenhauer 1970, 65.

Chapter 1

1. "Theodore" means "gift of god." "Twombly" derives from a place-name, but the American artist Cy Twombly was known for "writing" on the canvas rather than drawing or painting.

2. At this point, Cleverbot is pretty old and primitive, but you can still interact with it at www.cleverbot.com/. A good podcast about Cleverbot is available at www.radiolab.org/story/137407-talking-to-machines/.
3. Although it is a rare phenomenon, more than a few individuals have become so absorbed playing video games that they have actually died (from heart attack, thrombosis, thirst, or some combination). See Parkin 2015.
4. Rousseau 1967, 66 (my translation).

Chapter 2

1. Rousseau 1967.
2. Pope 2010.
3. The original storyboards depict the eye as that of the blade runner Holden, looking out on the city as he waits for his interview subject to arrive. But director Ridley Scott has said that he purposefully de-personalized the eye so that it is unclear to whom it belongs (Kolb 1991).
4. "Blade runners" are a special order of police who hunt fugitive androids known as "replicants." Marder's intelligent analysis (1991) makes the interrogation the "primal scene" of the film, one that is repeated, in some sense, over and over—but this neglects the characterless shots of the city and the eye that precede it. It is the human/representation binary (and not the human/replicant contrast) that in fact comes prior, both logically and in the order of the film itself.
5. Dick 1996 [1968], 112–28.
6. The reading of *Blade Runner* as an exemplar of postmodernism was given an influential early exposition by Giuliana Bruno (1987), who is explicit in applying Frederic Jameson's theories and terminology to the film.
7. The "final cut" box set contains five different versions of the film: an early workprint, the original 1982 US release, the 1982 international release, the "director's cut" released in 1992, and the "final cut" released in 2007. The director's cut restores some lost footage and disposes of most of voiceover as well as the closing shots of Deckard and Rachel escaping the city. The final cut has the same basic structure as the director's cut but includes some reshot and reedited materials that "fix" various continuity and editing problems in the earlier versions.
8. In drawing on the book to help explicate the film, I am not trying to undercut the distinctiveness of the film, which apart from being in a different medium has different authors and diverges from the novel in many ways. Rather, I am trying to use Dick's material to bring out some elements of the film that are genuinely present but that much of the rhetoric around the film (including Scott's) has tended to obscure.

   Accounts of the production indicate that the different views of Deckard were there from the beginning. The authors of the screenplay, in line with the book, always took Deckard to be human, as did actor Harrison Ford, who felt that the audience would not relate to his character as a non-human. Whether Scott originally was certain that Deckard was a replicant or only wanted to leave the audience in doubt is not clear. In any case, the producers of the original film removed the ambiguity that Scott wanted to create (Deckard's unicorn daydream). When Scott got control of the film for the subsequent releases, he reintroduced the cut footage and became more vocal about insisting that Deckard clearly was a replicant. See Turan 1992 and Sammon 1996.

9. "Rachael" originally means "ewe" in Hebrew. The name "Roy Batty" (in the novel it is spelled Roy Baty) is probably derived from Robot (Ro-Bot = Roy Baty).
10. Norris 2013.
11. Ibid., 27, 33.
12. Ibid., 33–34.
13. Ibid., 23.
14. Mulhall 1994, 90.
15. Norris 2013, 34.
16. An early reviewer actually pointed out that, since Roy himself seems particularly fearless, the line in this context doesn't make much sense (Ed Blank, qtd. in Kolb 1990, 23).
17. This is how Deckard first describes them: "Replicants are like any other machine. They're either a benefit or a hazard. If they're a benefit, it's not my problem."
18. I am not saying, of course, that the experience of encountering subjectivity is, or could be, the *only* pleasure of cinema. However, I would claim that it is the principal one, as evidenced by the dearth of commercial films that lack relatable central characters. I do not have space here to consider the case of television, but I think my point could be reinforced from that perspective: although there is much more non-narrative television than film, most of it contains a different kind of encounter with subjectivity.
19. Rousseau 1960, 79ff.
20. Ibid., 81.
21. Cavell 1979, 377; cf. Hegel 1977, 111ff.
22. Berger 1988.
23. Rousseau 1968, 82.
24. "When the social tie begins to slacken and the state to weaken, when particular interests begin to make themselves felt and sectional societies begin to exert an influence over the greater society, the common interest becomes corrupted and meets opposition; voting is no longer unanimous; the general will is no longer the will of all; contradictions and disputes arise; and even the best opinion is not allowed to prevail unchallenged. In the end, when the state, on the brink of ruin, can maintain itself only in an empty and illusory form, when the social bond is broken in every heart, when the meanest interest impudently flaunts the sacred name of the public good, then the general will is

silenced: everyone, animated by secret motives, ceases to speak as a citizen any more than as if the state had never existed" (Rousseau 1968, 150).

25. Rousseau 1968, 149.
26. Green 2010, Manin 1997.
27. See Urbinati 2006 and Landemore 2008. I thank Lisa Disch for calling my attention to the issues discussed in the preceding paragraphs.
28. In addition to Mulhall 1994 and Norris 2013, see Desser 1991, Gwaltney 1991, and Barlow 1991. See also Alessio 2005 and Barringer 1997.

Chapter 3

1. Mouffe 2000, 43.
2. Ibid., 4.
3. "The normative aspect of law can thus be obliterated and contradicted with impunity by a governmental violence that—while ignoring international law externally and producing a permanent state of exception internally—nevertheless still claims to be applying the law" (Agamben 2005, 87).
4. "Judges are people of violence. Because of the violence they command, judges characteristically do not create law, but kill it. Theirs is the jurispathic office" (Cover 1993a, 155). See also Cover 1993b.
5. "Again and again, we have seen how the politics of foreignness are driven by failed efforts to insist on the unity of the nation or the demos and to insure that the supplement of foreignness only supports regimes that are, however, always also unsettled by it" (Honig 2001, 117).
6. "As democracy, modern mass democracy attempts to realize an identity of governed and governing, and thus it confronts parliament as an inconceivable and outmoded institution. If democratic identity is taken seriously, then in an emergency, no other constitutional institution can withstand the sole criterion of the people's will, however it is expressed. . . . Democracy seems fated then to destroy itself in the problem of the formation of the will" (Schmitt 1985, 15, 28).
7. See, for example, Lubet 2000, Pearson 2009, Pippin 2010.
8. Honig 2009, 37.
9. Ibid., 24.
10. Ibid., 130.
11. Ibid., 13. Mouffe also suggests that we remain within the paradox, but I find her suggestions for how to do so very vague.
12. See Johnson 2005. Many names and details in the story are altered in the movie. "Tom Doniphon" is originally "Bert Barricune" and is more clearly Ransom's enemy, while Liberty Valance is an abstraction who hardly appears in the story at all. "Ransome Foster" (in the story) is also a stranger character,

while Barricune is less heroic than Doniphon. The story is powerful, but also largely personal and (intensely) psychological, with the political implications left in the background.

13. Ford personally bought the rights to the story from Johnson and commissioned the script, which is credited to James Warner Bellah and Willis Goldbeck but undoubtedly had a great deal of input from Ford (Palmer 2009).
14. Pippin 2010, 96. See also Sarris 1975, 75ff., which is an excellent discussion on many levels.
15. Pippin 2010, 89.
16. Stanley Cavell called the film "the fullest expression of the knowledge of the cost of civilization" (1979, 58). I have also benefitted from reading, among others, Anderson 1981, 178ff.; McBride and Wilmington 1975, 175ff.; Bohnke 2001, 47–63. Levy 1998 is also a wonderful resource. The literature on John Ford is, of course, vast, and I cannot touch on all of it here.
17. The significance of some names in the film is obvious. Others require explanation (discussed later), and others are harder to fathom, above all "Doniphon"—a name so confusing that it was often, understandably, rendered as "Donovan" by early critics and film writers. Without a character list, which does not appear in the credits, one would have to notice the name spelled out over a stockade and displayed only briefly in the movie to be sure of the correct spelling. Alexander Nehamas has suggested to me that, by combining the Latin *donum* with the Greek *phontes,* we can understand "Doniphon" as the equivalent of "death-giver," which does suit Wayne's role in the film.
18. A point recognized by some more than others. See, for example, Westal 2009: "The film doesn't endorse this [print-the-legend] point of view, it merely acknowledges the inevitability that beautiful lies will always overpower brutal or drab truths." See also Bogdanovich 1978: "Ford prints the fact" (34). Gallagher, closer to the truth, says Ford prints "both the facts and the legend" (1986, 409).
19. Gilles Deleuze has it precisely backward when he writes (in his brief comments on the film) that "what counts for Ford is that the community can develop certain illusions about itself" (1986, 147).
20. With its large Mexican American population, its status as a territory in the late nineteenth century, and its battles between farmers and ranchers, it seems most like Arizona, Colorado, or possibly New Mexico. The "Picketwire" river, much mentioned in the film, is an actual alternate name for the Purgatoire River in southeastern Colorado. One scene, however, shows a (crudely painted) American flag with 38 stars, which would put the date of the main action after 1876, when Colorado joined the Union as the thirty-eighth state (and before 1889, when then next four states were admitted, none of which had a significant Latino population). From all this, it seems clear that no particular state was intended. The time of the initial "present" is not clearly indicated in the

film; in Johnson's story, it is named in the opening sentence as 1910 (Johnson 2005, 25, 49).

21. Some writers have tried to understand the "valance" part of Liberty's name as if it were synonymous with "valence" and meant "value" or "level." The principal meaning of "valance" is that of a decorative drapery, and Liberty is surely given to an ostentatious display of himself (e.g., the whip). Tracy Strong suggests that we read the name to mean "the appearance of liberty." But while the *Oxford English Dictionary* says that "valance" is also an obscure word for courage, it also sounds a great deal like the "violence" to which the character is very prone.
22. Doniphon calls Stoddard "pilgrim" throughout the film—a usage that became such a staple of John Wayne impersonators it can be hard to remember that it is distinctive only to this film and serves a particular purpose.
23. Earlier reviews called attention to this question and considered it a flaw in the plot. See Coe 1962 and Weiler 1962.
24. Pippin 2010, 76.
25. The answer is surely not authenticity. Shot largely indoors in an atmosphere that has been described as claustrophobic, *Liberty Valance* is a highly unrealistic western. Given that the location of the town is unspecified, it hardly needs to be a place with Spanish speakers present.
26. Pompey is often remembered (debatably) as the last defender of the Republic against Caesar. Woody Strode was part of Ford's regular "company" of actors, had been a football star at UCLA and professionally, and had played the heroic lead in Ford's 1960 film *Sergeant Rutledge*.
27. Yet there are no Native Americans in this scene, or any other in the movie, which (given the fact that they are a regular presence in Ford's westerns) must be a deliberate choice. I would hazard that the point is that Blacks and Hispanics (and women), though second-class citizens, are still citizens, whereas the exclusion of Native Americans is so total that to pretend otherwise would be a falsehood. Ford's 1964 film *Cheyenne Autumn* has long been read as a kind of apology to Native Americans for their ongoing exclusion from the American polity.
28. Some of these points are made in a fine discussion of the scene in Pearson 2009, 178.
29. The scene also contains comic reminders of the language barriers that the Mexican American students face.
30. Pateman 1988, 2. See, more generally, her chapter 4.
31. Sedgwick 1990, 94, 15. See also Sedgwick 1985.
32. Bourdieu 2001, 53.
33. Carson 1986, 16.
34. The cactus rose has been used throughout the film to symbolize love.

35. For a slightly different perspective, see Darby 1996, which contains many fine, close readings of individual scenes.
36. Bourdieu 2001, 30.
37. See Gallagher 1986, 408–13; Pippin 2010, 86–96. This is hardly a universal view. Ransom's character is viewed much more positively in the excellent interpretation of the film presented in McBride and Wilmington 1975, 175–89.
38. Girard 1977, 1.
39. This point is well made in Roche and Hosle 1994, a brilliant reading of the film with a great eye for detail.
40. See Dienstag 2006, ch. 1.
41. In his excellent book on hypocrisy, David Runciman draws the distinction as follows: "Hypocrites who know what they are doing at least know that what they are doing is hypocrisy. But hypocrites who lack the sense that they are responsible for the part that they are playing can also lack a sense of responsibility for its consequences" (2008, 11). I thank Melissa Lane for suggesting this book to me and noting the similar points we are making.
42. Arendt 1958, 175.
43. Ibid., ch. 5.
44. Mouffe 2000, 100.
45. See Barr 2011. I thank one of my anonymous readers for noting the importance of this.
46. *Liberty Valance* opened to tepid reviews: "Film Offers Big Names, Tired Topic" was the title of a 1962 short notice in the *Chicago Daily Tribune*. Even the initial review in *Film Quarterly* was negative (and remarkably unperceptive): "The stock materials are terribly worn by now . . . very laxly made" (Callenbach 1963–1964, 43). Brendan Gill wrote in *The New Yorker* that it was "a parody of Mr. Ford's best work" (qtd. in Davis 2014, 310). The film barely covered its costs at the box office despite the presence of Wayne and Stewart, who were two of the biggest stars at the time and had never before appeared together (for costs and box office figures, see Gallagher 1986, 500). By the end of the 1960s, however, the film was generally referred to as John Ford's last great work. Indeed, one critic, writing in 1971, already complains that the film is not worthy of the "extravagant claims" being made on its behalf (Baxter 1971, 164).
47. Girard 1977, 99.

Chapter 4

1. I neither need nor want to take a position here on what the ultimate nature of evil is. I briefly survey some accounts of it here, but the point is that *whatever* one's theory of evil, the question of whether and how it should be represented, cinematically or politically, is a difficult and peculiar one.

2. Of course, Hollywood movies are not uniformly optimistic, as the other chapters of this book attempt to establish. One might think of the horror genre, in particular, as a continuous confrontation with questions of evil. But insofar as Hollywood is associated with "happy endings" and other "uplifting" sentiments, it is easy to understand how rejection of such themes can seem like opposition to Hollywood per se.
3. *Europa* was released in the United States under the title *Zentropa* to avoid confusion with the film *Europa Europa*, which appeared the previous year. But it was released elsewhere as *Europa*, and most von Trier filmographies now refer to it by that title.
4. The group began as a stunt that von Trier and Vinterberg cooked up for a conference celebrating 100 years of cinema. According to Vinterberg, they wrote the Dogma 95 Manifesto and the Vow of Chastity in forty-five minutes (http://www.dogme95.dk/the-vow-of-chastity/). Eventually, they formed a board with others to "certify" films, including their own, as conforming to Dogma rules, a practice they eventually discontinued. See www.dogme95.dk/dogma-95/ .
5. See www.dogme95.dk/the-vow-of-chastity/ . Clearly, the Dogma "rules" bear some relation to the anti-illusionism of radical film theory of the 1960s and 1970s. See Rodowick 1994, ch. 1. There is a large debate about the Dogma group, its intent, its seriousness, its meaning, and its consistency. I cannot respond to this literature here but see a fine discussion in Rooney 2015, ch. 4.
6. Or both: an initial target of Dogma 95 was New Wave French cinema, which they felt had become part of the bourgeois edifice it once appeared to criticize.
7. Thus, it opposed cinematic as opposed to theatrical techniques—the use of fictional characters and settings, which were the province of the screenwriter, not the director. See Apostolidis 2015 for a discussion of von Trier's "theatricality" in *Dogville*.
8. See www.dogme95.dk/dogma-95/ .
9. These techniques may also suggest the influence of the "modernist" critics of conventional popular filmmaking. See Rodowick 1994, ch. 1.
10. Von Trier's earlier film *The Element of Crime* (1984) also depicts itself as a product or effect of hypnosis.
11. Von Trier later named his own film company Zentropa. The word plays on "zoetrope," a nineteenth-century device that is often cited as a predecessor to cinema, as well as on the name of an actual train company (Mitropa).
12. "Katherine Hartmann," played by Barbara Sukowa, looks and sounds like Katherine Hepburn and is often called "Kate," as Hepburn was. What's more, her role as the wayward daughter of a wealthy family is a typical Hepburn role. Yet "Hartmann" was the family name of von Trier's true biological father, something his mother had only revealed to him shortly before *Europa* was made. Von Trier had been raised to believe that his father was a secular Danish Jew and was more than a little surprised to learn that he was instead the son

of a Catholic German. The film could thus be read as a wayward relative reacquainting himself with his German family.

13. The *Werwolfs* was a real Nazi guerilla organization that did carry out some sabotage and assassinations after the German surrender; it was largely suppressed by the end of 1945.
14. "Kessler" means "kettlemaker" or "coppersmith," but in Yiddish, it also means "a man who lives with his in-laws," which is not far from what is happening in the film.
15. The passage being quoted is Revelations 3:16.
16. As Lori Marso has argued, claims of about Von Trier's misogyny are, at the least, exaggerations and simplifications (Marso 2015).
17. James 1899.
18. Kateb 2002, 496.
19. Ibid., 496–97. I have reversed the order in which these two sentences appear.
20. There is, in fact, an asteroid named Melancholia. It shows no signs of striking Earth. See ssd.jpl.nasa.gov/sbdb.cgi?sstr=5708+Melancholia#content.
21. See, for example, Lippe 2012.
22. Peterson (2013) collects several examples of this approach before offering his own, more interesting reading.
23. From the press kit (!) to *Melancholia*: "In a way, the film does have a happy ending . . . If it could happen in an instant, the idea appeals to me. . . . So if the world ended and all the suffering and longing disappeared in a flash, I'm likely to press the button myself" (www.festival-cannes.com/assets/Image/Direct/042199.pdf, 3, 6).
24. Indeed, in the early modern period, Robert Burton, in his famous *Anatomy of Melancholia* (2001), associated melancholics with werewolves, who, he said, haunted graveyards at night, in the light of the moon. The connection between melancholy and lycanthropy is intelligently discussed by Rossello 2012. Among other things, Rossello describes how melancholy, in the seventeenth century, was still understood physiologically but had a wide meaning that potentially covered many conditions, including the believed-by-some mental disturbance of lycanthropy.
25. See, for example, Schopenhauer 1970, 51–54.
26. See Marso 2015 for a more nuanced discussion of this complicated question.

Chapter 5

1. See Plaugic 2018 and Lupis 2017.
2. In their original form, the *Up* series may well have been intended to conform to John Grierson's early ideas (so influential in Britain) about documentary as a work of "social responsibility," "citizenship," and "a screen interpretation of the

modern world." I will be arguing in effect that they ended up carrying out that responsibility in a way neither Grierson nor their directors originally intended. See Grierson 1966, 145–51.

3. As a helpful reviewer pointed out to me, the *Up* series is not the first "reflexive" documentary of its kind (see Ruby 1977; Henley 2009). In highlighting its virtues here, I do not intend to enter into the large set of arguments about whether documentary film is either generically better than fiction films at representation or more "realistic." The potential for staging and manipulation in documentary films is well known. Still, the *Up* series, I hope to establish, does display a particular mode of representation to a remarkable degree. For discussion of the documentary genre, see Corner 1996 and Nichols 1991.
4. *Seven Up!* was directed by Paul Almond—all the subsequent films have been directed by Michael Apted, who worked as an assistant on *Seven Up!* and chose the participating children. Apted is generally recognized as the motivating force who turned the original film into a series and has maintained it through a variety of producers and funding sources.
5. The narrator speaks of twenty children, and indeed, we see at least that many in group shots. However, only fifteen (ten boys and five girls) speak directly to the camera, and only fourteen of these (one girl is omitted) are followed in later films.
6. This is the only film without "Up" in the title—the rest of the films are named *21 Up*, *28 Up*, and so on. The title may also reflect the fact that there are fourteen participants. If one groups the middle-class participants with the rich ones, then that would make seven more privileged subjects and seven less privileged ones.
7. While most of the subjects have participated continuously, John does not appear in *28 Up* and *42 Up*, Peter does not appear in any film between *28 Up* and *56 Up*, Symon skipped *35 Up*, and Charles (himself a documentary filmmaker at the BBC) has not appeared in any film since *21 Up*. In later films, the non-participants' profiles are diminished or eliminated.
8. Apted described the process in an interview with *Fresh Air's* Terry Gross ("Michael Apted, Aging with the '7 Up' Crew" 2013).
9. See Nicholas Hitchon's comments ("Michael Apted, Aging with the '7 Up' Crew" 2013).
10. See www.rogerebert.com/reviews/great-movie-the-up-documentaries-1985.
11. In the most recent films, some earlier clips are discreetly labeled with a date or title—usually to prevent confusion.
12. See www.cinemetrics.lv/bordwell.php.
13. Suzy in *56 Up*.
14. See, for example, Mead 2013 and Winerip 2013.
15. Although it is no longer a common position, attacks on democracy for the low quality of its decisions remain popular in some quarters. See, for example, Bell 2015 and Brennan 2016.

16. In an interview, Apted has spoken of having to work to become less judgmental over the years. Listening to his questions, however, one doubts that he has made much headway.
17. Nietzsche 1974, 104. This is also Gadamer's point in *Truth and Method* (1975)—that understanding can only come from the "fusing" of past and present horizons.
18. Beckett 1983, 3.
19. Rousseau 1968, 141.

Chapter 6

1. Borges 1999, 325. This point is certainly acknowledged—and, indeed, made central—by much film theory. See Cavell 1971, ch. 1; Kracauer 1960; Bazin 1967.
2. Tracy Lord in *The Philadelphia Story*.
3. Heidegger 1977, 3–35.
4. See Baudry 2004.
5. Gadamer 1975, 137.
6. Ibid., 137.
7. Ibid., 137.
8. Ibid., 140.
9. See Dienstag 2017.

BIBLIOGRAPHY

Agamben, Giorgio. *State of Exception*. Chicago: U of Chicago P, 2005.

Alessio, Dominic. "Redemption, 'Race,' Religion, Reality, and the Far-Right: Science Fiction Film Adaptations of Philip K. Dick." *The Blade Runner Experience: The Legacy of a Science Fiction Classic*. Ed. Will Brooker. London: Wallflower, 2005, pp. 59–78.

Almond, Gabriel, and Sidney Verba. *The Civic Culture*. Princeton: Princeton UP, 1963.

Alonso, Sonia, John Keane, and Wolfgang Merkel, eds. *The Future of Representative Democracy*. Cambridge: Cambridge UP, 2011.

Anderson, Lindsay. *About John Ford*. London: Plexus, 1981.

Anker, Elisabeth R. *Orgies of Feeling: Melodrama and the Politics of Freedom*. Durham: Duke UP, 2014.

Ankersmit, F. R. *Aesthetic Politics: Political Philosophy Beyond Fact and Value*. Stanford: Stanford UP, 1996.

Apostolidis, Paul. "'Young Americans': Ranciere and Bowie in *Dogville*." *Theory and Event*, vol. 18, no. 2, 2015. https://muse.jhu.edu/article/578629.

Arendt, Hannah. *The Human Condition*. Chicago: U of Chicago P, 1958.

Aristotle. *On Poetry and Style*. New York: Bobbs-Merrill, 1958.

Badiou, Alain. *Cinema*. Cambridge: Polity Press, 2013.

Barlow, Aaron. "Philip K. Dick's Androids: Victimized Victimizers." *Retrofitting Blade Runner*. Ed. Judith Kerman. Bowling Green: Bowling Green State U Popular P, 1991, pp. 76–89.

Barr, Alan P. "*The Man Who Shot Liberty Valance* Inhabits Film Noir." *Western American Literature*, vol. 46, no. 2, 2011, pp. 162–79.

Barrett, Estelle, and Barbara Bolt. *Carnal Knowledge: Towards a "New Materialism" Through the Arts*. London: I. B. Tauris, 2012.

Barringer, Robert. "Blade Runner: Skinjobs, Humans, and Racial Coding." *Jump Cut: A Review of Contemporary Media,* vol. 41, 1997, pp. 13–15, 118.

Baudry, Jean-Louis. "Ideological Effects of the Basic Cinematographic Apparatus." *Film Theory and Criticism*. Ed. Leo Braudy and Marshall Cohen. 6th ed. Oxford: Oxford UP, 2004 [1974], pp. 355–65.

Baxter, John. *The Cinema of John Ford*. New York: A. S. Barnes, 1971.

Bazin, Andre. *What Is Cinema*? Trans. Hugh Gray. 2 vols. Berkeley: U of California P, 1967, 1971.

Beckett, Samuel. *Worstword Ho*. New York: Grove Press, 1983.

Being There, Dir. Hal Ashby, Lorimar Film Entertainment, 1979.

Bell, Daniel A. *The China Model: Political Meritocracy and the Limits of Democracy*. Princeton: Princeton UP, 2015.

Benjamin, Walter. "The Work of Art in the Age of Mechanical Reproduction." *Illuminations*. New York: Schocken, 1968, pp. 217–52.

Berger, John. "Why Look at Animals?" *About Looking*. New York: Random House, 1988.

Blade Runner. Dir. Ridley Scott. The Ladd Company, Shaw Brothers, and Warner Brothers, 1982. DVD, Video.

Blade Runner (The Director's Cut). Dir. Ridley Scott. Warner Home Video, 1992. DVD, Video.

Blade Runner (The Final Cut). Dir. Ridley Scott. Warner Home Video, 2007. DVD.

Bogdanovich, Peter. *John Ford*. Berkeley: U of California P, 1978.

Bohnke, Michael. "Myth and Law in the Films of John Ford." *Journal of Law and Society,* vol. 28, no. 1, March 2001, pp. 47–63.

Borges, Jorge Luis. *Collected Fictions*. Trans. Andrew Hurley. New York: Penguin, 1999.

Bourdieu, Pierre. *Masculine Domination*. New York: Polity Press, 2001.

Brennan, Jason. *Against Democracy*. Princeton: Princeton UP, 2016.

Bruno, Giuliana. "Ramble City: Postmodernism and *Blade Runner*." *October,* vol. 41, Summer 1987, pp. 61–74.

Burton, Robert. *The Anatomy of Melancholy*. New York: New York Review of Books, 2001.

Byron, John. "Replicants R Us: The Crisis of Authenticity in *Blade Runner*." *Sydney Studies,* vol. 34, 2008, pp. 41–62.

Callenbach, Ernest. "*The Man Who Shot Liberty Valance* and *Donovan's Reef* by John Ford; Willis Goldbeck." *Film Quarterly,* vol. 17, no. 2, Winter 1963–1964, pp. 42–44.

Carson, Anne. *Eros: The Bittersweet*. Princeton: Princeton UP, 1986.

Cavell, Stanley. *The World Viewed*. Cambridge: Harvard UP, 1971.

Cavell, Stanley. *The Claim of Reason*. Oxford: Oxford UP, 1979.

Cavell, Stanley. *Pursuits of Happiness*. Cambridge: Harvard UP, 1981.

Cavell, Stanley. *Cities of Words*. Cambridge: Harvard UP, 2004.

Coe, Richard L. "Way in Egg Role." *Washington Post*, April 21, 1962, p. 9.

Comolli, Jean-Luc, and Jean Narboni. "Cinema/Ideology/Criticism." *Film Theory and Criticism*. Ed. Braudy and Cohen. Oxford UP, 2004 [1969]. https://muse.jhu.edu/article/32663.

Connolly, William E. "Film Technique and Micropolitics." *Theory and Event*, vol. 6, no. 1, 2002a.

Connolly, William E. *Neuropolitics: Thinking, Culture, Speed*. Minneapolis: Minnesota UP, 2002b.

Corner, John. *The Art of Record: A Critical Introduction to Documentary*. Manchester: Manchester UP, 1996.

Cover, Robert. "Nomos and Narrative." *Narrative, Violence, and the Law: The Essays of Robert Cover*. Ed. Martha Minow, Michael Ryan, and Austin Sarat. Ann Arbor: U of Michigan P, 1993a, pp. 95–172.

Cover, Robert. "Violence and the Word." *Narrative, Violence, and the Law: The Essays of Robert Cover*. Ed. Martha Minow, Michael Ryan, and Austin Sarat. Ann Arbor: U of Michigan P, 1993b, pp. 203–38.

Darby, William. *John Ford's Westerns: A Thematic Analysis, with a Filmography*. Jefferson: McFarland, 1996.

Davis, Ronald L. *John Ford: Hollywood's Old Master*. Norman: U of Oklahoma P, 2014.

De Lauretis, Teresa. *Alice Doesn't: Feminism, Semiotics, Cinema*. Bloomington: Indiana UP, 1984.

Deleuze, Gilles. *Cinema 1*. Minneapolis: U of Minnesota P. 1986.

Deleuze, Gilles. *Cinema 2*. Minneapolis: U of Minnesota P. 1989.

Desser, David. "Race, Space, and Class: The Politics of the SF Film from *Metropolis* to *Blade Runner*." *Retrofitting Blade Runner*. Ed. Judith Kerman. Bowling Green: Bowling Green State U Popular P, 1991, pp. 110–23.

Dick, Phillip. *Do Androids Dream of Electric Sheep?* New York: Del Rey, 1996 [1968].

Dienstag, Joshua Foa. *Pessimism: Philosophy, Ethic, Spirit*. Princeton: Princeton UP, 2006.

Dienstag, Joshua Foa. *Cinema, Democracy and Perfectionism*. Manchester: Manchester UP, 2016.

Dienstag, Joshua Foa. "The Example of History and the History of Examples in Political Theory." *New Literary History*, vol. 48, no. 3, 2017, pp. 483–502.

Disch, Lisa. "Toward a Mobilization Conception of Democratic Representation." *American Political Science Review*, vol. 105, no. 1, 2011, pp. 100–14.

Disch, Lisa. "Democratic Representation and the Constituency Paradox." *Perspectives on Politics*, vol. 10, no. 3, 2012a, pp. 599–616.

Disch, Lisa. "The Impurity of Representation and the Vitality of Democracy." *Cultural Studies*, vol. 26, no. 2–3, 2012b, pp. 207–22.

Disch, Lisa. "Beyond Congruence." *Political Representation: Roles, representatives and the Represented*. Ed. Marc Bühlmann and Jan Fivaz. London: Routledge, 2016, pp. 85–98.

Disch, Lisa, Mathijs van de Sande, and Nadia Urbinati. *The Constructivist Turn in Political Representation*, Edinburgh: Edinburgh UP, 2019.

Dovi, Suzanne. *The Good Representative*. Oxford: Blackwell Publishing, 2012.

Dovi, Suzanne. "Hanna Pitkin, 'The Concept of Representation.'" *The Oxford Handbook of Classics in Contemporary Political Theory*. Ed. Jacob T. Levy. Oxford: Oxford UP, 2015. https://www.oxfordhandbooks.com/view/10.1093/oxfordhb/9780198717133.001.0001/oxfordhb-9780198717133-e-24.

Eisenstein, Sergei. "The Dramaturgy of Film Form." *Film Theory and Criticism*. Ed. Leo Braudy and Marshall Cohen. 6th ed. Oxford: Oxford UP, 2004.

Erens, Patricia, ed. *Issues in Feminist Film Criticism*. Bloomington: Indiana UP, 1990.

Europa. Dir. Lars von Trier, Nordisk Film, 1991.

"Film Offers Big Names, Tired Topics." *Chicago Daily Tribune*, April 27, 1962, p. B14.

Francavilla, Joseph. "The Android as Doppelgänger." *Retrofitting Blade Runner*. Ed. Judith Kerman. Bowling Green: Bowling Green State U Popular P, 1991, pp. 4–15.

Frank, Jason. *Constituent Moments*. Durham: Duke UP, 2010.

Gadamer, Hans-Georg. *Truth and Method*. New York: Continuum Publishing, 1975.

Gallagher, Tag. *John Ford: The Man and His Films*. Berkeley: U of California P, 1986.

Garsten, Bryan. "Representative Government and Popular Sovereignty." *Political Representation*. Ed. Ian Shapiro, Susan Stokes, and Elizabeth Wood. Cambridge: Cambridge UP, 2010, pp. 90–110.

Girard, René. *Violence and the Sacred*. Baltimore: The Johns Hopkins UP, 1977.

Green, Jeffrey Edward. *The Eyes of the People: Democracy in an Age of Spectatorship*. Oxford: Oxford UP, 2010.

Grierson, John. *Grierson on Documentary*. Ed. Forsyth Hardy. Berkeley: U of California P, 1966.

Gwaltney, Marilyn. "Androids as a Device for Reflection on Personhood." *Retrofitting Blade Runner*. Ed. Judith Kerman. Bowling Green: Bowling Green State U Popular P, 1991, pp. 32–39.

Hegel, G. W. F. *Hegel's Phenomenology of Spirit*. Oxford: Oxford UP, 1977.

Heidegger, Martin. *The Question Concerning Technology and Other Essays*. New York: Harper & Row, 1977.

Henley, Paul. *The Adventure of the Real: Jean Rouch and the Craft of Ethnographic Cinema*. Chicago: U of Chicago P, 2009.

Her. Dir. Spike Jonze, Warner Bros. Pictures, 2013.

Hobbes, Thomas. *Leviathan*. Cambridge: Cambridge UP, 1991.

Holleran, Scott. "Close-Up: Dan Ford on John Wayne and John Ford." *Box Office Mojo*. June 21, 2007. www.boxofficemojo.com/features/?id=2338&p=.htm.

Honig, Bonnie. *Democracy and the Foreigner*. New Jersey: Princeton UP, 2001.

Honig, Bonnie. "Between Decision and Deliberation: Political Paradox in Democratic Theory." *American Political Science Review*, vol. 101, no. 1, 2007, pp. 1–17.

Honig, Bonnie. "Antigone's Laments, Creon's Grief: Mourning, Membership, and the Politics of Exception." *Political Theory*, vol. 37, no. 1, 2009, pp. 5–43.

Honig, Bonnie. *Antigone, Interrupted*. Cambridge: Cambridge UP, 2013.

Honig, Bonnie. "Public Things." *Political Research Quarterly*, vol. 68, no. 3, 2015, pp. 623–36.

Hopper, Hedda. "Ford Keeps Ahead of Young Producers." *Los Angeles Times*, May 8, 1962, p. C14.

James, William. *On Some of Life's Ideals*. New York: Henry Holt, 1899.

Jerslev, Anne. "Dogma 95, Lars von Trier's *The Idiots*, and the 'Idiot Project.'" *Realism and "Reality" in Film and Media*. Ed. Anne Jerslev. Copenhagen: Museum Tusculanum Press, 2002, pp. 41–66.

Johnson, Dorothy M. *The Man Who Shot Liberty Valance*. Helena: Riverbend, 2005 [1953].

Kant, Immanuel. *Critique of the Power of Judgment*. Trans. Paul Guyer and Eric Matthews. Cambridge: Cambridge UP, 2000.

Kateb, George. "The Adequacy of the Canon." *Political Theory*, vol. 30, no. 4, 2002, pp. 482–505.

Kolb, William M. "*Blade Runner*: An Annotated Bibliography." *Literature Film Quarterly*, vol. 18, no. 1, 1990, pp. 19–64.

Kolb, William M. "*Blade Runner*: Film Notes." *Retrofitting Blade Runner*. Ed. Judith Kerman. Bowling Green: Bowling Green State U Popular P, 1991, pp. 154–77.

Kozinski, Jerzy. *Being There*. New York: Harcourt Brace Jovanovich, 1970.

Kracauer, Sigfried. *Theory of Film: The Redemption of Physical Reality*. Princeton: Princeton UP, 1960.

Landemore, Hélène. "Is representative democracy really democratic? Interview of Bernard Manin and Nadia Urbinati." *Books and Ideas.net*, 2008. https://booksandideas.net/Is-representative-democracy-really-democratic.html.

Levy, Bill. *John Ford: A Bio-Bibliography*. Westport: Greenwood Press, 1998.

Lippe, Richard. "Lars Von Trier and *Melancholia*." *CineAction*, vol. 86, Winter 2012, pp. 62–63.

Lubet, Steven. "The Man Who Shot Liberty Valance: Truth or Justice in the Old West." *UCLA Law Review*, vol. 48, no. 2, 2000, pp. 353–74.

Lupis, J. C. "The State of Traditional TV." *Marketing Charts*, December 13, 2017. www.marketingcharts.com/featured-24817.

Macpherson, C. B. *The Life and Times of Liberal Democracy*. Oxford: Oxford UP, 1977.

Manin, Bernard. *The Principles of Representative Government*. Cambridge: Cambridge UP, 1997.

Manin, Bernard, and Nadia Urbinati. "Is Representative Democracy Really Democratic?" Interview by Helene Landemore. *Books and Ideas.net*, 2009. https://booksandideas.net/IMG/pdf/20080327_manin_en.pdf.

Mansbridge, Jane. "Rethinking Representation." *American Political Science Review*, vol. 97, no. 4, 2003, pp. 515–28.

Mansbridge, Jane. "A 'Selection Model' of Political Representation." *Journal of Political Philosophy*, vol. 17, no. 4, 2009, pp. 369–98.

Mansbridge, Jane. "Clarifying the Concept of Representation." *American Political Science Review*, vol. 105, no. 3, 2011, pp. 621–30.

Mansbridge, Jane. "Recursive Representation in the Representative System." HKS Working Paper No. RWP17-045, 2017. https://papers.ssrn.com/sol3/papers.cfm?abstract_id=3049294.

Marder, Elissa. "*Blade Runner's* Moving Still." *Camera Obscura*, vol. 9, no. 3, 1991, pp. 88–107.

Marso, Lori. "Must We Burn Lars von Trier?: Simone de Beauvoir's Body Politics in *Antichrist*." *Theory and Event*, vol. 18, no. 2, 2015.

McBride, Joseph, and Michael Wilmington. *John Ford*. Boston: Da Capo, 1975.

Mead, Rebecca. "What '56 Up' Reveals." *The New Yorker*, January 9, 2013. https://www.newyorker.com/culture/culture-desk/what-56-up-reveals.

Melancholia. Dir. Lars von Trier, Zentropa Entertainments, 2011.

Metz, Christian. *The Imaginary Signifier*. Bloomington: Indiana UP, 1977.

"Michael Apted, Aging with The '7 Up' Crew." *Fresh Air*. NPR, February 5. 2013. Radio. www.npr.org/2013/07/26/205760044/michael-apted-aging-with-the-7-up-crew.

Mouffe, Chantal. *The Democratic Paradox*. Brooklyn: Verso, 2000.

Mulhall, Stephen. "Picturing the Human (Body and Soul): A Reading of *Blade Runner*." *Film and Philosophy*, vol. 1, 1994, pp. 87–104.

Mulvey, Laura. "Visual Pleasure and Narrative Cinema." *Screen*, vol. 16, no. 3, 1975, pp. 6–18.

Nichols, Bill. *Representing Reality: Issues and Concepts in Documentary*. Bloomington: Indiana UP, 1991.

Nietzsche, Friedrich. *The Gay Science*. New York: Vintage Books, 1974.

Nietzsche, Friedrich. *The Portable Nietzsche*. New York: Penguin, 1977.

Norris, Andrew. "'How Can It Not Know What It Is?': Self and Other in Ridley Scott's *Blade Runner*." *Film-Philosophy*, vol. 17, no. 1, 2013, pp. 19–50.

Palmer, Daryl W. "The Spokesman: Dorothy M. Johnson's 'The Man Who Shot Liberty Valance' and Infinite Reference." *Theory and Event*, vol. 12, no. 4, 2009. https://muse.jhu.edu/article/368572.

Panagia, Davide. "Why Film Matters to Political Theory." *Contemporary Political Theory*, vol. 12, no. 1, 2013, pp. 2–25.

Parkin, Simon. *Death by Video Game: Tales of Obsession from the Virtual Frontline*. London: Serpent's Tail Press, 2015.

Pateman, Carole. *Participation and Democratic Theory*. Cambridge: Cambridge UP, 1976.

Pateman, Carole. *The Sexual Contract*. Stanford: Stanford UP, 1988.

Pearson, Sidney A., Jr. "It Is Tough to Be the Second Toughest Guy in a Tough Town: Ask the Man Who Shot Liberty Valance." *Print the Legend: Politics, Culture, and Civic Virtue in the Films of John Ford*. Ed. Sidney A. Pearson, Jr. Lanham: Lexington, 2009, pp. 169–88.

Peterson, Christopher. "The Magic Cave of Allegory: Lars von Trier's *Melancholia*." *Discourse*, vol. 35, no. 3, 2013, pp. 400–22.

Pippin, Robert B. *Hollywood Westerns and American Myth: The Importance of Howard Hawks and John Ford for Political Philosophy*. New Haven: Yale UP, 2010.

Pitkin, Hannah Fenichel. *The Concept of Representation*. Berkeley: U of California P, 1967.

Plato. *The Republic of Plato*. New York: Basic Books, 1968.

Plaugic, Lizzie. "Domestic Movie Theater Attendance Hit a 25-Year Low in 2017." *The Verge*, January 3, 2018. www.theverge.com/2018/1/3/16844662/movie-theater- attendance-2017-low-netflix-streaming.

Plotke, David. "Representation is Democracy." *Constellations*, vol. 4, no. 1, 1997, pp. 19–34.

7 Plus Seven. Dir. Michael Apted, Granada Television, 1970.

Pope, Richard. "Affects of the Gaze: Post-Oedipal Desire and the Traversal of Fantasy in Blade Runner." *Camera Obscura: Feminism, Culture, and Media Studies*, vol. 25, no. 1, 2010, pp. 69–95.

Rancière, Jacques. *Hatred of Democracy*. London: Verso, 2006.

Rehfeld, Andrew. *The Concept of Constituency: Political Representation, Democratic Legitimacy and Institutional Design*. Cambridge: Cambridge UP, 2005.

Rehfeld, Andrew. "On Representing." *The Journal of Political Philosophy*, vol. 26, no. 2, 2018, 216–39.

Rickman, Gregg. "Philip K. Dick on *Blade Runner*: 'They Did Sight Stimulation on My Brain.'" *Retrofitting Blade Runner*. Ed. Judith Kerman. Bowling Green: Bowling Green State U Popular P, 1991, pp. 103–107.

Roche, Mark W., and Vittorio Hosle. "Vico's Age of Heroes and the Age of Men in John Ford's Film *The Man Who Shot Liberty Valance*." *Clio*, vol. 23, no. 2, 1994, pp. 131–51.

Rodowick, D. N. *The Crisis of Political Modernism: Criticism and Ideology in Contemporary Film Theory*. Berkeley: U of California P, 1994 [1988].

Rooney, Monique. *Melodrama and Plasticity in Contemporary Film and Television*. London: Rowman and Littlefield, 2015.

Rossello, Diego. "Hobbes and the Wolf-Man: Melancholy and Animality in Modern Sovereignty." *New Literary History*, vol. 43, no. 2, 2012, pp. 255–79.

Rousseau, Jean-Jacques. *Politics and the Arts: Letter to M. D'Alembert on the Theatre*. Ithaca: Cornell UP, 1960.

Rousseau, Jean-Jacques. *Lettre à D'Alembert*. Paris: Garnier-Flammarion, 1967.
Rousseau, Jean-Jacques. *The Social Contract*. New York: Penguin, 1968.
Ruby, Jay. "The Image Mirrored: Reflexivity and the Documentary Film." *Journal of the University Film Association*, vol. 29, no. 4, 1977, pp. 3–11.
Runciman, David. "The Paradox of Political Representation." *The Journal of Political Philosophy*, vol. 15, no. 1, 2007, pp. 93–114.
Runciman, David. *Political Hypocrisy*. Princeton: Princeton UP, 2008.
Sammon, Paul M. *Future Noir: The Making of Blade Runner*. London: Orion, 1996.
Sarris, Andrew. *The John Ford Movie Mystery*. Indianapolis: Indiana UP, 1975.
Saward, Michael. *The Representative Claim*. Oxford: Oxford UP, 2010.
Schiller, Friedrich. *On the Aesthetic Education of Man*. New Haven: Yale UP, 1954.
Schopenhauer, Arthur. *Essays and Aphorisms*. New York: Penguin, 1970.
Schmitt, Carl. *The Crisis of Parliamentary Democracy*. Trans. Ellen Kennedy. Cambridge: MIT Press, 1985.
Schwartz, Nancy. *The Blue Guitar: Political Representation and Community*. Chicago: U of Chicago P, 1988.
Sedgwick, Eve Kosofsky. *Between Men*. New York: Columbia UP, 1985.
Sedgwick, Eve Kosofsky. *Epistemology of the Closet*. Berkeley: U of California P, 1990.
Seven Up!. Dir. Paul Almond, Granada Television, 1964.
Shapiro, Michael. "A Philopoetic Engagement: Deleuze and *The Element of Crime*." *Theory and Event*, vol. 18, no. 2, 2015. https://muse.jhu.edu/article/578628.
Shetley, Vernon, and Alissa Ferguson. "Reflections in a Silver Eye: Lens and Mirror in *Blade Runner*." *Science Fiction Studies*, vol. 28, no. 1, 2001, pp. 66–76.
Singer, Peter. *Animal Liberation*. New York: Harper Collins, 1975.
Students for Democratic Society. *The Port Huron Statement*. New York: Students for a Democratic Society, 1962.
The Man Who Shot Liberty Valance. Dir. John Ford, Paramount Pictures Corp, 1962.
The Complete Up Series, Dir. Michael Apted, First Run Features, 2013.
Tormey, Simon. *The End of Representative Politics*. Cambridge: Polity Press, 2015.
Turan, Kenneth. "Blade Runner 2." *Los Angeles Times*, September 13, 1992. https://www.latimes.com/archives/la-xpm-1992-09-13-tm-1537-story.html.
21 Up. Dir. Michael Apted, Granada Television, 1977.
28 Up. Dir. Michael Apted, Granada Television, 1984.
35 Up. Dir. Michael Apted, Granada Television, 1991.
49 Up. Dir. Michael Apted, Granada Television, 2005.
56 Up. Dir. Michael Apted, ITV Studios, 2012.
Urbinati, Nadia. *Representative Democracy: Principles and Genealogy*. Chicago: U of Chicago P, 2006.
Urbinati, Nadia, and Mark E. Warren. "The Concept of Representation in Contemporary Democratic Theory." *Annual Review of Political Science*, vol. 11, 2008, pp. 387–412.

Weiler, A. H. "Man Who Shot Liberty Valance Opens at Capitol Theater." *New York Times*, May 24, 1962, p. 29.

Westal, Bob. "The Man Who Shot Liberty Valance." *Bullz-Eye.com*, 2009. www.bullz-eye.com/mguide/reviews_1962/the_man_who_shot_liberty_valance.htm.

Williams, Melissa S. *Voice, Trust, and Memory: Marginalized Groups and the Failings of Liberal Representation*. Princeton: Princeton UP, 1998.

Wilson, Eric G. "Moviegoing and Golem-Making: The Case of *Blade Runner*." *Journal of Film and Video*, vol. 57, no. 3, 2005, pp. 31–43.

Winerip, Michael. "Taking Family Seriously in 'Up' Series." *New York Times*. https://www.nytimes.com/2013/01/07/booming/56-up-shows-generations-commitment-to-family.html.

Wolin, Sheldon. *Democracy Incorporated*. Princeton: Princeton UP, 2008.

Wollen, Peter. "Godard and Counter Cinema: *Vent d'est*." *Afterimage*, vol. 4, Fall 1972, pp. 6–17.

INDEX

For the benefit of digital users, indexed terms that span two pages (e.g., 52–53) may, on occasion, appear on only one of those pages

Figures are indicated by *f* following the page number

www.ingramcontent.com/pod-product-compliance
Ingram Content Group UK Ltd.
Pitfield, Milton Keynes, MK11 3LW, UK
UKHW020226250726
13967UKWH00001B/222

9 780190 067724